Garden House Diaries

by Ruth Tomalin

★

NOVELS
All Souls
The Garden House
The Spring House
Away to the West
Long Since

★

VERSE
Threnody for Dormice
Deer's Cry

★

BIOGRAPHY
W.H.Hudson

★

FOR CHILDREN
The Daffodil Bird
The Sea Mice
A Green Wishbone
A Stranger Thing
The Snake Crook
Gone Away
Another Day
Little Nasty
A Summer Ghost

★

As Ruth Leaver
Green Ink
The Sound of Pens

Garden House Diaries

Life on a country estate 1930-1945

Edited, with Foreword and Afterword,

by

RUTH TOMALIN

QUERCUS PRESS

Copyright © Ruth Tomalin and the Estates of

T.E. Tomalin, Elspeth Tomalin,
John Woolfries and Tony Tomalin, 2003

Quercus Press, 10 Pegasus Court,

Eastbourne, BN21 3UP

All rights reserved

The moral right of the authors has been asserted.

ISBN 0-9545182-0-9

Typeset by MusicPrint, Warblington

Printed and bound by RPM Print & Design, Chichester

CONTENTS

Foreword .... *vii*

1 In the gardens — T.E. Tomalin 1

2 In the woods — Ruth Tomalin 37

3 In wartime — Elspeth Tomalin 70

Appendix 1 121
Prisoner of war, 1945

Squadron Leader John Woolfries, RAF

Appendix 2 127
Looking back: Normandy, 1944/1951

Major Tony Tomalin, London Welsh Regiment

Afterword 132

T.E. Tomalin, AHRHS (1880–1954), gardener, writer and lecturer, was born on a country estate, Oakwood in Kent, where his father was manager. He learned his craft in famous gardens, including Burghley in Lincolnshire and Middleton Park in Oxfordshire. From 1907 he was head gardener to the Earls of Bessborough in Co. Kilkenny, Ireland, and later at Stansted Park in Sussex.

"His reputation as a grower, exhibitor and judge of fruits was the highest. From these gardens he staged magnificent exhibits at the Royal Horticultural Society's Autumn shows. He was awarded many cups and trophies, and in 1952 an exhibit of fruits from Stansted Park, comprising 73 varieties of Apples, as well as Grapes and Pears, was awarded the Gordon Lennox Cup by the Royal Horticultural Society. In 1949 he was appointed, with the late Mr Thomas Hay, to judge the first show promoted by the British Army of the Rhine, in Germany. He devoted his whole life to horticulture." – *The Gardeners' Chronicle,* 20th February 1954.

In 1943 the Society had conferred on him an Associateship of Honour. He served on RHS Committees, held a popular series of gardening classes at Portsmouth in the 1930s, and contributed for many years to the horticultural Press, but declined editorial offers which might have entailed a change to town life.

Entries for "In the gardens" are from the Gardeners' Chronicle feature The Week's Work, to which he contributed for 18 consecutive years.

Elspeth Tomalin (1892-1963), from a Scottish Border farming family, grew up at Bessborough, where her father was land steward. She went to school in Scotland and trained as a teacher at a Dublin college; but, like many women of her day, married early and never held a post. Later she gave frequent talks to Women's Institutes and served on WI Committees.

Ruth Tomalin was born in Bessborough Gardens and grew up at Stansted. In wartime she worked in the women's land army, and as a staff reporter on the Portsmouth Evening News.

Foreword

In the 1930s the walled garden at Stansted, ringed with trees, lawns and orchards, was a combined market garden, training school and miniature research unit. As today, it was also a 'pleasure ground' and a thriving nature reserve.

There were gardeners about all day, from the veteran who, at his own steady pace, looked after the flower-beds and shrubberies near the mansion, to the boy who scrubbed flower-pots, weeded and swept paths, and sometimes stole five minutes behind a yew hedge with the Boy's Own Paper. Nesting birds would sit quietly while men worked close by. A barn owl took over a garden pigeon-cote. Swallows came year after year to house eaves, outbuildings and the Chapel porch. Red squirrels had their dreys in the tall redwood trees of the arboretum, visiting the old orchard for cherries and hazel nuts. Hares jumped the park fences to gambol on the lawns at dawn. Colonies of bee orchises and autumn lady's-tresses were protected. Meadows around were still 'wildflower meads', filled in spring with cowslips and green-winged orchises.

In August, when the garden smelled of flowers and ripening fruit, the butterflies and moths had their high season, preyed on by spotted flycatchers. Morning glories flowered on the walls of a small paved garden, their seeds munched by climbing fieldmice. September brought goldfinches for more flower seeds, while departing swallows mustered in flocks around the mansion, as they do today. In winter birds stripped the berried shrubs, and green woodpeckers quartered the lawns for ants.

Beyond the gardens and park, in the forest of beech, oak, fir and Spanish chestnut, the cries of many roosting pheasants mingled at dusk with the first owl calls. Rabbits swarmed, red squirrels raced in the treetops, fallow deer roamed and dormice were active at sunset and in the early morning, foraging in briars, brambles and hazels: beautiful little creatures, yellowish-buff with fuzzy tails and large dark eyes. They rested by day with their young in round summer nests of woven grasses, and hibernated in leafy nests under tree roots, their sleep so deep that they could be carried home undisturbed and protected for the winter, then released in April. Various reasons have been put forward for their disappearance at the end of the decade; but at Stansted 'loss of habitat' may be ruled out. Their old haunts remain, awaiting their hoped-for reinstatement.

Keepers reared and took care of the game, as they had done for centuries. In the twelfth century, when this was a royal hunting ground, a falconer named Silvester was 'looking after the King's birds in the park.'* That name was still on the register at Forest Side school.

A team of foresters carried on the old woodland crafts: trimming the undergrowth, clearing the wreckage of autumn gales for firewood, planting young trees from the forest nursery and shielding them with wire netting from damage by deer and rabbits. Chestnut copses were cut in rotation, like the hazel copses, and made into fencing. Legend has it that Mr Churchill, visiting Stansted in wartime, noticed these chestnut 'mats' and suggested their use on the beaches at the D-Day landings. In the weeks before that day the western fringe of the forest became a vast military camp, and woodland rides hid a great arsenal of tanks and army vehicles.

Meanwhile another ancient craft had returned to the scene, as charcoal burners worked near by. Sapling trees were cut into brands and piled into square iron kilns in an open ride, lighted at the centre through a trapdoor. The foreman spent his nights in a caravan beside the kilns, in case of a flare-up that might endanger the product and the blackout. Twenty-four hours' smouldering turned the wood into charcoal, used in making silk for parachutes.

* *A Place In The Forest* by the Earl of Bessborough (1958)

I

In the Gardens

1933-1939

T.E. Tomalin

<u>2nd January</u>

<u>Strawberries</u> Pot strawberries required for Easter dessert may be brought under cover now. Probably the soil in the pots will be very wet and this should be allowed to dry somewhat before pricking the surface and top-dressing with a little fresh compost. The vinery or peach house will afford suitable accommodation for the plants, especially if a shelf near the glass is available.

<u>5th January</u>

<u>Mid-winter flowers</u> The Winter Sweet, Chimonanthus fragrans, gives earlier and more abundant blossom when trained against a south or west wall, and, with Lonicera fragrantissima, should be planted near the windows of the dwelling-house. Both have, this season, been in flower since mid-December, and their fragrance has well repaid the forethought of the planter. They should be spur-pruned after they have finished flowering in early spring.

Jasminum nudiflorum – an old-fashioned flower which, when cut, makes a delightful winter decoration – and Garrya elliptica, which at this season bears a mantle of yellowish-green catkins, both contrast well with dark evergreen foliage. In the shrubbery a group of the Chinese Witch Hazel, Hamamelis mollis, covered with orange-yellow blossoms, and Viburnum fragans, with blush-white, sweet-smelling flowers, are of great charm. Iris unguicularis has seldom flowered more generously than this winter. Beginners usually err in being too generous to this plant, which flowers freely in rather poor soil. An additional inducement to its flowering is the shearing off of over-luxuriant leaves to half their length at midsummer. The varieties alba, with white flowers, and speciosa, with larger and more deeply coloured blossoms, add further interest to a group of these plants.

11th January

Reminders Before the advent of really severe weather it is well to give a look round in case any young or semi-tender shrubs are still unprotected. Dry bracken packed around the base and through the lower branches, with a good covering of spruce boughs to keep it in place, will afford sufficient protection to most shrubs or plants.

The returfing of bare patches on the lawns may be undertaken during mild weather when conditions are too wet for work on the ground. The earlier this can be done the better chance will the new turf have of becoming closely knit to the rest before spring arrives with drying winds.

If Winter Returns Heavy snow is often responsible for the loss of branches from conifers of mature age, and workers armed with long poles should be sent round after exceptional snow-storms to dislodge this extra weight from the trees before a rising wind completes the mischief.

18th January

Seeds and seed-sowing All stocks of home-saved seeds should be cleaned and packeted, for the time for sowing many kinds is now at hand. Having then examined the seeds in store and estimated further requirements, the order for these should be sent immediately.

Among plants that require a long season of growth, the seeds of which should now be sown, are East Lothian Stocks, Antirrhinums, Delphiniums, Hollyhocks, Penstemons and, for their ornamental foliage, such plants as Melianthus major and the silvery-grey Cineraria maritima and Centaurea ragusina.

28th January

The Fruit Store Try to maintain equable and cool conditions

in the fruit room at this season. A fairly low temperature is best for late apples and pears, although when the latter are ready they respond to warming, like claret, with an enhanced flavour. All decayed and spotted fruits should be removed, but the less these fruits are moved about the longer they will keep. The ideal to aim at is to examine each one carefully when storing and to reject all pecked or damaged fruits, to pack the sound ones closely together so as to reduce evaporation and consequent shrivelling, and then to leave them alone until each variety becomes mature, when it should be used without delay.

Bush Apples and Pears The leading shoots of last season's growth should now be pruned back to about one-third of their length, always cutting to a wood bud pointing in the direction in which each branch should extend, in order to balance the tree. The centre of the tree should be kept open, and the main branches encouraged to grow at even distances apart. All side growths should have been pruned back during the summer, but if this was not done they should now be cut back to within two or three eyes of the base.

Canker The tendency to canker in young trees on heavy soils has been mentioned, and although root-pruning will check this, the only cure is to cut out all cankered patches with a sharp knife, the wounds so made being dressed with Stockholm tar. It is very gratifying to the keen fruit-grower to observe the clean new bark which will form over the cleanly cut wounds in a season, and in time will re-encircle a branch that was almost surrounded by canker.

Some standard trees of Cox's Orange Pippin treated by the writer over twenty years ago in Ireland were almost despaired of at that time, but they completely grew out of the tendency to canker, and last autumn bore splendid crops of clean, well-coloured fruits.

4th February

Planting Fruit Trees Although November is perhaps the most favoured month in which to plant fruit trees, it is not always possible to get the work completed then. If the preparation of the ground has been thorough, spring planting, even so late as the middle of March for apples, may be quite successful, although fruit trees planted in the spring require more care and watchfulness during periods of dry weather in their first season.

It is a golden rule never to plant fruit trees too deeply; the soil mark on the stem will indicate the correct depth at which to cover the roots. It is inadvisable also to add farmyard or stable manure at planting time, for it will result in the formation of rank, sappy growths, often barren of fruit buds, and a ready prey to canker on wet soils. When the trees have formed good heads and are cropping freely, they should be manured regularly and generously.

A little extra attention in the preparation of the site for each tree will be well repaid by results, especially in the case of choice dessert apples and pears. Some extra drainage material, in the form of a six-inch layer of broken bricks, with a layer of good turf grass-side downwards over this, will form a good foundation for the lower roots to rest on and to root into. This will ensure a good start, which is half the battle in forming a profitable fruit plantation.

8th February

Winter colour Beauty of colouring in trunk, branch and stem is apparent in the reddish-brown bole of Sequoia sempervirens, in the silver birches, the golden willow, in the warm red stems of Cornus sanguinea, and the yellow stems of C. stolonifera var. flaviramea, while among the Rubus species the white-stemmed R. biflorus and R. giraldianus may he effectively associated with the red, hirsute stems of the Wineberry.

Among berry-bearing plants of winter interest mention must be made of three species of Cotoneaster, C. rotundifolia, C. frigida and C. serotina. The latter is very late in colouring, while the fruits of the two former species are eschewed by the birds, which strip most of the other species in autumn.

Close on the heels of the first snowdrops, the purple and lavender-blue buds of the earlier crocus species, C. imperati and C. sieberi, are pushing well above the short grass in which they are set.

<u>9th February</u>

<u>Standard Fuchsias and Heliotropes</u> Old standard plants used for summer planting out of doors should now be pruned closely and stood in a temperature such as that in a newly-started vinery, where they may be encouraged by regular sprayings to break into new growth.

<u>Melons</u> Where a light and well-heated house is available, melon seeds may now be sown for an early crop. The seeds should be sown in small pots, lightly covering them with sifted loam, which should be sufficiently moist to render watering unnecessary until they have germinated. The pots should be plunged in a propogating case in a warm house with a temperature of 65° to 70° until the seedlings come through the soil, when they should be placed on a shelf in a house where a similar temperature may be maintained. In the meantime a hotbed should be prepared, consisting of tree leaves and stable manure, well consolidated and fairly near the glass, in readiness for the young plants.

Warm moist conditions are essential to success with melons and must be maintained throughout their growth, except at flowering time, when a drier atmosphere during the forenoon will assist pollenation, and again when the fruits are ripening, when atmospheric moisture must be reduced gradually.

The Early Peach House Early peaches and nectarines will now be in flower, and hand pollenation will be necessary to ensure that fruits set. For this purpose, when bees are not working, nothing is better than a couple of rabbits' tails on the end of a light bamboo. Advantage should be taken of every bright day for this operation. Keep the atmosphere in the house dry to ensure a free movement of pollen until the brush has been used, after which the trees may be given a light syringing. A rise in temperature will be beneficial in promoting steady growth.

18th Febuary

Propagation If it is thought desirable to increase the stock of any of the varieties of bush fruits, some of the best shoots should be collected from those pruned off, and carefully labelled. Choose for them a piece of firm ground on a sheltered border, cut a vertical trench five inches deep, and place the cuttings upright, six inches apart. The soil should then be returned to the trench and made thoroughly firm about them.

Spraying An operation which should no longer be postponed is that of spraying all peach and nectarine trees on walls with Burgundy mixture for the prevention of leaf-curl.

Clematises Although some of the large-flowered hybrids do not take kindly to all soils and situations, generally, all do fairly well in those districts where the wild clematis or "traveller's joy" flourishes. Towards the end of February is a good time to plant, choosing a partially shaded position, or one where some low-growing bush will intercept the midday sun from the fleshy surface roots.

Border Chrysanthemums Stock plants which have been wintered in cold frames should be kept well ventilated to encourage the production of sturdy cuttings. Generally speaking, the beginning of March is early enough to begin propogating these, when the seedlings may be rooted in boxes of sandy soil in a close house or frame with a temperature of 45° to 50°. Cuttings taken too early are apt to become hard before planting-out time, and never "break" so freely as those planted from cutting boxes to ground without any check. If, however, certain varieties have already developed shoots of cutting length, these should be rooted with a view to taking off their tops to strike again, in March or early April. The first-rooted batch may then be planted early in a sheltered part of the reserve garden, whence they may be lifted when in bud to furnish any parts of the flower borders where earlier flowering subjects may perhaps have left a space.

4th March

Strawberries The best time to plant strawberries is early August, and if the ground for the new bed is thoroughly trenched and manured now, it may be cropped with early potatoes. These will be lifted during July, and the necessary working and cultivation will leave the ground in excellent tilth for the young strawberry runners.

Alpine Strawberries A border of Alpine strawberries is valuable in prolonging the season of this fruit far into the autumn months. They will fruit as annuals if sown in gentle heat in February, and the young plants gradually hardened off and planted out in May. The ripe fruits are greatly esteemed for dessert, with the addition of sugar and cream, and they also make a preserve of a peculiarly piquant flavour.

7th March

Annual Flowers To see these at their very best a deeply cultivated and well-manured border with a sunny aspect should be reserved for them. This can be a very charming feature of the flower garden, and the idea may be extended so as to embrace various features, such as blends of one colour or another. When planning such borders it should be remembered that some of the most beautiful annuals are comparatively short-lived in flower, while other kinds will continue to flower until frost puts an end to their display. The various kinds in these two categories should occupy separate borders, and, to name a few examples, in the first group I would place the Clarkias and Godetias, Lavateras and Candytuft, while the more lasting group would include the branching Larkspurs, Lupinus hartwegii and L. mutabilis, the annual Chrysanthemums, Arctotis, Nigella, Alonsoas and Eschscholtzias.

Mignonette No English flower garden can be considered complete in summer-time without a bed of Mignonette, for its fragrance is equally welcome whether in the garden or cut and disposed in bowls about the house. Mignonette flourishes in well cultivated soil containing lime or mortar-rubble and made thoroughly firm before sowing. Early thinning is most important, and the young seedlings should ultimately be spaced at one foot apart. If the plants are prevented from seeding they will continue to grow and flower over a long period, but successional sowings from March until the end of May is the best way of ensuring a continuous supply throughout the summer.

11th March

Protection From Frost Covering materials may soon be required to protect the early-flowering apricots and peaches during frosty nights. Covers of Hessian canvas, so arranged that they can be drawn like curtains over the trees at night and removed early in the morning, form the best protection for apricots. Although it is true that the less these trees have to be covered the better, it is not wise to be in too great a hurry to expose the blossom to full sunshine after a night of severe frost; if the trees face in an easterly direction, it is better to allow the covers to remain in position until about 10 a.m. For peach and nectarine trees in flower, a double thickness of ordinary garden netting, hung well clear of the trees, affords sufficient protection, and serves not only to guard the flowers from frost but also to temper the easterly winds to the tender young foliage.

A small hook near the top of each pole will enable the nets to be hitched up on fine mild days, and give easy access to the flowers for pollenating. Fine dry conditions have favoured hand pollenation with the rabbit's tail on those days when a fresh easterly wind kept the bees in their hives. We use a separate instrument for each kind of fruit, and regularly use them for peaches, apricots, plums, pears and sweet cherries. The crossing of the different varieties of each kind of fruit is of course helpful in obtaining a good set of fruits, and is essential with all the sweet cherries, and with many of the best dessert pears, which are known to be self-sterile.

18th March

Figs In cold districts where outdoor figs have to be given protection during the winter months, the covering may now be removed, and the trees pruned before the sap becomes too active. This is a very suitable time to plant fig trees, and the best position is at the foot of a wall facing south or west, although here in the south we gather splendid fruits from trees on an east-facing wall.

The most reliable variety for outdoor planting is Brown Turkey, but White Marseilles is also worth trying for its excellent flavour.

25th March

Grafting In many gardens, trees of apples and pears may be found which, although healthy in root and stem, fail to yield satisfactory crops, while others may be of inferior varieties. Such trees may now be headed back and top-grafted with some of the more up-to-date varieties, with better prospects of an earlier return than would be the case where young trees are planted.

It is important that the stock should be rather in advance of the scion in seasonal growth, therefore the scions should have been selected some weeks ago, and heeled in deeply in a shaded position to keep them dormant. The lower three inches of the scion should be cut into a thinly tapering wedge, and a vertical cut made right through the bark of the stock, long enough to take the wedge-shaped end of the scion. The bark on each side of the vertical cut should be carefully loosened, just sufficiently to admit the scion, using a smooth wedge-shaped implement, such as the handle of a budding knife, and then carefully closed over the scion, taking care that the inner bark of both stock and scion are in contact, for it is upon this particular that success in grafting depends.

The junction should then be closely bound with insulating tape, which is more effective than raffia in excluding air, and, being adhesive, is much handier to use, for it may be cut off at any point and no tying is involved. Moreover, very little grafting wax need be used, just a slight coating over the cut portion of the stock to complete the operation.

Grafts should be examined periodically to ensure that the union remains airtight. It is a wise precaution to affix a long cane to the stock, to extend beyond the end of each scion, to protect the young shoots from damage by alighting birds.

4th April

Herbaceous Borders Last year, owing to pressure of other work, three herbaceous borders had to be completely replanted after 1st April, and the planting was a complete success, the various groups making good growth and covering the ground well before flowering time. The plants included Heleniums in several varieties; Asters of the amellus, cordifolius, novae-angliae and novi-belgii types, Rudbeckias, Phloxes, Campanulas, Coreopsis, Helianthuses,

Lobelias, Montbretias, Salvia nemorosa and many other kinds. The secret of success in late spring planting lies in thorough cultivation and enrichment of the ground, in careful division of such plants as Heleniums, Asters and others of similar habit into small healthy portions, and in regular after-care, watering, hoeing and staking.

The Loganberry This prolific and easily grown member of the Rubus family may still be planted, if it can be done at once and a little extra care is expended on the plants for a few weeks until they become well established. Many people dismiss the loganberry as a coarse fruit of harsh flavour, but when bottled in syrup and kept for six months it is improved immensely, and furnishes a welcome dish during the fruit scarcity of early spring.

13th April

The Flower Beds Now that all Tulips and other spring-flowering bulbs are well above the ground, the surface soil should be stirred between them. This treatment will encourage the growth of carpeting plants such as Myosotises, Aubrietia, Alyssum saxatile, Cheiranthus allionii, which will quickly spread out and cover the ground.

Ivy This is a most useful climbing plant for aspects where more interesting evergreen climbers might not be a success. If the leaves are closely shorn during early April, the plants will soon show fresh young leafage. There are many varieties with very beautiful leaves, and a collection of these may be a decorative feature in winter.

22nd April

Apricots The fruits being set, the trees will now be in active growth, and timely attention to disbudding and stopping the young growths will encourage the formation of fruiting spurs, and obviate the necessity for much of the winter pruning which is so harmful to apricot trees. If this work is persevered with during the summer, the trees should be well furnished with fruit buds for next season.

If too many fruits have set, thinning may proceed concurrently with attention to the young growths; but, as with all stone fruits, thinning should be done cautiously, and in at least three operations.

First, remove only those badly placed fruits which have not room to develop properly. A week or so later, a few more should be taken off, if all are swelling evenly. Finally, after the stoning period has safely passed – for it is at this period that many stone fruits fail and drop off – the last thinning may be done.

<u>Reminders</u> The stock of nets should be overhauled and those in need of repair attended to on the first rainy day, when stakes and pegs also may be prepared, and all accessories put in readiness to prevent delay and loss when crops need quick protection.

Stocks of packing materials should also be examined, for the season will by now give some indication of the fruit-grower's requirements in punnets, chip-baskets, boxes, wood-wool etc.

<u>27th April</u>

<u>The Water Garden</u> Nymphaeas and other aquatic plants may now be divided and replanted. The safest method of establishing choice varieties of Water Lilies is by planting separate crowns in moss-lined baskets filled with a mixture of good loam and old cow manure. In natural waters and ponds one may simply attach a weighty stone to each crown, to anchor it to the mud at the bottom.

The Water Hawthorn gives a succession of fragrant white flowers, often until very late autumn, and its floating seeds attach themselves to any convenient anchorage, forming new colonies – sometimes too generously. The pink Butomus umbellatus, with rush-like leaves, is a delightful plant for shallow water, and the floating Arum, Calla palustris, will flower either when anchored by its roots or when floating at large over the surface.

At the water-side, just in the water, the sweet-scented Rush may be established, while at the edge positions should be found for plants such as Myosotis palustris, Mimulus and Caltha palustris. Irises such as I. orientalis, I. sibirica and I. kaempferi give wonderful reflective effects from the opposite bank, and are even more striking when associated with plants such as the Gunneras, Eulalia (Miscanthus) japonica and Phormium tenax.

Peaches and Nectarines In common with the cherries and plums, these have made a wonderful floral picture in the cold orchard house, and, unless time was found to thin out the blossoms, much thinning has now to be done.

2nd May

The Spring Flower Beds are now approaching their most attractive period. Now is the time to jot down ideas for next season's scheme of planting, for one of the joys of flower gardening lies in anticipation of the effect of some fresh arrangement or new idea in colour blending. Careful notes made now will at least ensure that this season's mistakes are not repeated.

11th May

Biennials Seeds of many hardy biennial flowers may now be sown out of doors in a sheltered border, preferably with a northern aspect. These include Wallflowers, Sweet Williams, Canterbury Bells, Cheiranthus allionii and Myosotis. Hardy perennials also may be grown under similar conditions, such as Foxgloves, Aquilegias, Iceland Poppies, Lupinus polyphyllus and Chelone barbata. If pricked out afterwards into nursery beds, they will provide good plants for autumn or early spring planting in the borders and woodland walks.

Half-hardy Climbers Many interesting and beautiful half-hardy climbing plants may be planted now. These are mostly of rapid growth and especially useful for covering blank spaces on trellises or pergolas while the permanent climbers are establishing themselves.

Ipomoea rubro-coerulea, with glowing purple convolvulus-like flowers, is suitable only for a warm sunny corner. Less exacting, and more rampant in growth, are Cobaea scandens, with large bell-shaped purple or greenish-yellow flowers; Eccremocarpus scaber, with tubular orange-coloured flowers, and Lophospermum scandens, with pink flowers. These should be sown in March, in a warm house, grown on in pots and gradually hardened off before planting out.

13th May

Strawberries Bedding down with clean straw should be carefully accomplished as soon as the first flowers open, the straw being well worked under the flower trusses.

Although neither practical nor necessary where acres of strawberries are grown in fields, in gardens protection from birds is very necessary. The best method is to enclose the whole strawberry bed with a framework of larch poles five feet high, with fourteen-gauge wire strained from post to post. Around the bottom, resting on the ground, three-inch wire netting of one-inch mesh should be fixed, and the string netting placed over the top and secured all round. Fixed in this way, a good string net will last at least eight years if stored dry, while the framework will remain so long as the bed lasts. A convenient doorway should of course be left at one corner.

25th May

Summer Bedding Far-seeing gardeners will have so arranged their spring displays that the hardier of the summer flowers will replace those whose spring flowers are over first, leaving beds still bright with the later Tulips, Cheiranthus etc for the more tender subjects, such as Heliotropes, which may not safely be put out until June.

Clearing The Beds Polyanthuses and Primroses may be divided and planted as groundwork for spring-flowering shrubs. If some of the best forms have been marked for seed-saving, these should be transplanted carefully. When the seeds are mature they should be ripened off and sown at once in a cold frame in a shaded position. A good strain of Myosotis can be perpetuated by shaking out the seeds from the lifted plants over a piece of cultivated ground. Seedlings in plenty will appear in a few weeks, and should be transplanted into nursery beds before they become too crowded.

Tulips and Daffodils should be lifted carefully and laid in trenches to complete their growth, with a view to replanting the Daffodils in grassland and the Tulips in the reserve garden for cut blooms next season.

29th May

The Vineries The grapes in the early vinery are now colouring, and a slight opening of the front ventilators each bright day will assist this process, besides enhancing their flavour. With the variety Madresfield Court, indeed, continuous front and top ventilation, combined with comfortably warm pipes at night, while the berries are colouring, is a safeguard against the skin-cracking to which this fine Grape is prone.

Late varieties, such as Alicante, Lady Downe's and Gros Colmar will now be passing out of flower, and their first thinning should start immediately. These varieties set thickly, and the bunches are very difficult to thin once they have become a congested mass of berries. The number of bunches each rod can carry successfully must depend on its length and vigour. All badly shaped and awkwardly placed bunches should be removed, leaving the better clusters evenly spaced over the vine.

The time-honoured practice is for the garden boy to try his 'prentice hand at thinning one or two of the discarded bunches, before being allowed to operate on those forming part of the crop.

10th June

Thinning the Fruits Many varieties of Apples have again set heavy crops, and drastic thinning will be necessary in order to produce an even crop of fine fruits. The final thinning, to one or two fruits to each cluster, must be deferred until after the "summer drop". Newly planted trees often show a tendency to overcrop in the first season, but to allow them to do so is fatal to their future well-being. No harm will result if they carry a few fruits, so long as satisfactory growth is being made at the same time.

22nd June

Rose Garden Chilly winds and low night temperatures are usually followed by an attack of aphis, and prompt measures should be taken to deal with this by spraying with a solution of nicotine and soft soap.

Rhododendrons and Azaleas Time should be found for the removal of dead flower heads. The prevention of seed-formation has a beneficial effect on growth, but the work must be carefully done or serious injury may result to the young growths proceeding from the base of the old flower head.

Auriculas The more vigorous forms of this charming group of Primulaceous plants are both effective and interesting when planted between the stones used for edging a garden path. They may be increased easily at this season by lifting and dividing strong plants into separate crowns, each with a piece of stem and root attached. These, if firmly dibbled into sandy soil and watered occasionally during dry weather, will quickly establish themselves and make good plants before next flowering season.

<u>27th June</u>

<u>The Iris Garden</u> The May- and June-flowering Bearded Irises have seldom given a finer display, and the comparative coolness of the period has prolonged their flowering. The best time for planting and transplanting is immediately after flowering is over. However, as an example of the amenability of these plants when misused, the writer, owing to force of circumstance, had to transplant some hundreds in April last year. These were, moreover, cleaned down to bare rhizomes with growing points. The flower buds were removed as they appeared, and the plants afterward made splendid growth, and this year have flowered magnificently.

In the choice of a site for Irises due regard must be given to shelter from wind when they are in flower. A suitable evergreen hedge may combine this purpose with a pleasing background for the tall yellow and white varieties.

<u>Seed-saving</u> Seeds of many spring-flowering plants are now ripe for gathering, though the later-flowering Primulas and Meconopses will not be ripe for a week or two yet. All germinate more freely if sown immediately the seeds are fully ripened.

For small quantities and rare varieties, carefully prepared pans of fine soil are most suitable, while for larger sowings a prepared bed in a shaded cold frame is most convenient. The soil should be finely sifted loam and leaf-soil or Sorbex peat, in equal parts, with a generous addition of sand. The bed should be carefully levelled and well watered before sowing, and the seeds just covered with a fine coat of similar material. Keep the frame close until the seedlings appear, after which air should be admitted freely; later, on fine nights, the lights may be removed to give the young seedlings the benefit of the night dews, replacing them in the daytime to give shelter from the midday sun and from drying winds.

29th June

The Herbaceous Borders Staking and tying are probably the most important tasks during the next few weeks, and nothing tends more to make or mar the effect than the manner in which this is done. Many plants may be effectively and unobtrusively supported by stout pea-sticks placed among and around the clumps. Taller plants are more securely held by driving stout stakes in and around each clump forming a group, and lacing a strand or two of soft fillis twine from stake to stake. If this is done with judgement no stake need be visible when the group is in flower.

Newly-sown Lawns The young grass on newly-sown lawns has made splendid growth since the recent rains began. If possible, the young growth should be cut first with a scythe. The lawn-mower should be set to cut as high as possible for the first few weeks, afterwards setting the cutter down gradually, a notch at a time, as the young grass tillers out and forms a sward.

Rough Grass Areas of grass in which bulbs are growing naturally may now be cut closely, for the bulb foliage will have withered. An exception may be made for another week or two, perhaps, of places where the autumn Crocuses have not yet quite ripened their foliage.

8th July

Summer Pruning The new growths on espalier and cordon trees of Apple and Pear growing on fences and walls should now be shortened to the fourth leaf, with the exception of the leading growths on each branch, which should be left to grow on, unless the tree has already filled its alloted space, in which case these may also be tipped. In order to avoid too severe a check to the tree, and consequent jeopardy to the crop, this work should be spread over a few weeks. Bush trees growing in the open may next be treated in the same manner.

Removal of superfluous lateral growth, by admitting air and sunlight to all parts of the tree, assists in the development of fruit buds on existing spurs, and also improves the quality and appearance of fruits. It is equally important for those trees which are not carrying full crops this season, for these usually make extra strong growth, and pruning will divert the tree's energies to the perfecting of next season's fruit buds.

Asters and Ten-week Stocks The latest batches of these should be planted before they have exhausted the soil in the boxes. If they are intended primarily for cut flowers, borders from which early potatoes and lettuces have been cleared often offer convenient space for them. Earlier plantations of these, and annuals of similar growth, should be staked in good time. Hazel suckers or apple prunings are very suitable, and one may pull them up and burn them with the exhausted plants – a hygienic practice which is often overlooked.

Green Cuttings Shoots of many shrubs and plants can be readily rooted at this season in pure sand in a close frame. Shrubs which are difficult to root from hard cuttings in autumn may be propogated in this manner, and will make sturdy plants, ready for nursery beds next spring.

13th July

Violets Spells of hot dry weather often prove very trying to Violets, and unless precautionary measures are taken against red spider this pest will quickly denude the plants of all healthy foliage. Regular spraying with weak soot-water will do much to discourage red spider, but, if the pest appears to be gaining on the plants, spraying once a week with a good paraffin emulsion is the most certain method of keeping them clean. Violets in active growth require a good soaking occasionally during dry periods, and this may be followed by a dusting with soot over the foliage while it is still damp. The following morning the ground between the plants should be stirred with the Dutch hoe, after which a mulch of old mushroom-bed manure or half-decayed leaves will conserve the moisture, and will greatly assist the plants during the critical months of July and August.

22nd July

Peaches and Nectarines The earlier varieties are now colouring, and to aid this process all overhanging leaves should be drawn away from the fruits and secured temporarily with raffia. Fruits which have not sufficient space to mature without risk of contact with the wire trellis or adjacent twigs should be raised slightly by placing a wooden label behind each one. Clean eight-inch labels are suitable, and may be used again and again if collected and stored.

During the ripening season the trees should be examined daily and fruits gathered as they ripen. In hot weather this should be done in the cool of the morning or evening, for there is then less risk of bruising than when the fruits are hot with sunshine; but during showery weather any opportunity must be seized when the fruits are dry.

Figs Birds are exceedingly fond of ripening figs, and if netting the whole tree is difficult the fruits may be protected with the hexagon netting bags sold for the purpose. As the fruits ripen in succession, and birds seldom touch them until they are becoming soft, the bags may be transferred to the next fruits as the first are gathered.

Perennial Lupins With a border devoted entirely to the hybrids of Lupinus polyphyllus a beautiful effect can be achieved, for the range of colour among the newer varieties is wide and affords scope for some wonderful blends and contrasts. They may also be happily associated with Bearded Irises, Paeonies, Anchusas and Oriental Poppies in a border reserved for such early-summer flowering plants, all of which become something of a problem in the mixed flower border in late summer; excepting perhaps some of the Irises and Paeonies, whose foliage has decorative value when the flowers are over.

This type of Lupin is easily increased by means of seeds, but such seedlings vary largely in both form and colour, and should be first planted in a nursery border, whence a selection may be made. Surer methods of perpetuating choice varieties are, however, available, for green cuttings can be taken from the base or stems of the old plants, while root cuttings form another ready means of increase.

29th July

Wasps Wasps and tits present a problem to the grower of choice fruits. Bags of hexagon netting are not infallible, because small birds can peck through the meshes. For two seasons we found ordinary biscuit bags very satisfactory for the protection of Pears and exhibition Apples, and then the tits discovered that those too could be pecked through with a little persistence, especially after rain – when, oddly enough, birds are often more mischievous than during dry weather. If bags of oiled silk could be produced cheaply enough the problem would perhaps be solved; but, failing these, stout new bags of greaseproof paper are perhaps the most practical means of protection. A smart lad can fix a surprising number of these in an hour.

1st August

The Herbaceous Borders are now at their gayest, and the removal of dead flowers, and provision of such extra supports as may be necessary, will greatly prolong the display. If any failures have occurred, or where perhaps an early-flowering group has become unsightly, the gap should be made good from the reserve border. Early-flowering Chrysanthemums, Asters and Phlox (decussata) may be moved successfully when in bud or flower if the work is carefully done, and a good ball of soil lifted with each plant. Other subjects often grown for this purpose are Humea elegans, standard and pyramid Fuchsias, Campanula pyramidalis and Japanese Liliums.

5th August

Early Dessert Apples The earliest varieties do not keep long in good condition and should therefore be used within a very few days of being gathered. Varieties such as Mr Gladstone, Beauty of Bath, St Everard and Lady Sudeley soon become mealy if kept for any length of time, although Irish Peach and Langley Pippin will remain in good condition rather longer. The trees should be gone over every two days and the fruits gathered as they become mellow.

Early varieties often fail to colour satisfactorily in cultivated ground, and it has been the writer's practice for over twenty years to lay them out on a closely mown plot of grass in the orchard, where the influence of night dews and showers, with sunshine, will soon colour them beautifully; and, if they are for market, will double their value. A dry day must of course be chosen for packing them when they have become coloured.

12th August

Early Pears All dessert varieties have a notoriously fleeting period of usefulness when ripe, and must therefore be closely watched lest their moment pass unnoticed. A heavy crop of

Jargonelle or Williams's Bon Chrétien, if all are gathered at once, will mature on or about the same day and must be used or disposed of immediately. For this reason it is advisable to gather them a few at a time, choosing those in the most forward stage at each gathering. The fruits should be laid out on wood-wool on a shelf in a cool fruit store, where they will ripen in a week or so. The right moment to gather Pears is when the stalk parts readily from its socket on lifting the fruit gently to a horizontal position, but the early varieties may be encouraged to part from the tree with rather more persistence than is advisable for the later ones, for, if these latter are gathered before their time, shrivelling will take place before ripening.

Early Dessert Plums and Gages usually ripen very irregularly, and, as they should be really ripe when gathered, the trees must be gone over two or three times a week to secure them as they approach their maximum of flavour.

Bulb Planting Daffodils which were lifted at the end of June, and have since been thoroughly ripened and stored, should now be planted as soon as a convenient site can be prepared. Some deterioration takes place in the bulbs with every week's delay in planting after the month of August. Among other bulbs and corms which are the better for early planting are the Crocus species, Scillas and Chionodoxas, which are suitable either for the lower terraces of the rock garden or for grassy slopes and glades, and at the foot of deciduous trees near a woodland walk. In similar positions, groups of Anemone blanda, A. nemorosa and its blue-tinted variety robinsonia, Leucojum vernum (the Spring Snowflake) and Grape Hyacinths (Muscari) will add beauty to the early months of the year. A crowbar may be necessary for making the holes, but a handful of fine soil should be dropped in for each bulb to rest on, and a little more added as a covering, after which the turf will soon close over the bulbs.

26th August

Late Peaches Trees on which the crop will hang for some weeks yet should be watered regularly and fed with liquid manure until the fruits begin to colour, after which clear water will suffice. If birds are troublesome the trees must be netted, and if earwigs abound these should be trapped by means of six-inch lengths of broad-bean stalk inserted here and there on the tree. These should be examined daily and the earwigs blown or shaken out into a tin containing a little paraffin, for they are most destructive of outdoor peaches, usually gnawing small holes near the base, whence rot starts and quickly renders the finest fruits useless.

Raising and Growing of shrubs and trees from seeds seems, oddly enough, to become more attractive the older one gets, for the impatience of youth is not proof against the delay in waiting for results which this fascinating pursuit entails. Collecting seeds from one's own shrubs and plants adds to their interest, and one of the most important details is the gathering at the right moment. This calls for constant watchfulness from now until late autumn.

The Cytisus family, Buddleias, Laburnums, Piptanthus nepalensis and Abutilon vitifolium are examples, among many others, of shrubs whose seeds will now, or soon, be ripe for gathering. They may be laid on trays and placed on a greenhouse shelf to ripen off, and should then be cleaned and packeted in readiness for sowing when the proper season arrives.

Lilium candidum Flourishing groups of this favourite Lily are best left undisturbed, but if for any reason transplanting becomes necessary it should be done before the end of August, for its resting period is short.

Summer Flower Beds Propogation of stocks for next season will be one of the flower gardener's most important tasks for the next few weeks. This is also a good time to go round, notebook in hand, seeking out the weak spots in the borders and noting how such places can be improved. In October most herbaceous plants can he lifted, divided and replanted, and each group to be so treated should now be carefully labelled as to variety and colour.

2nd September

Apples: Alternative Varieties Among dessert Apples, although one would advise perseverance with Cox's Orange Pippin even on the most uncongenial soils, there are others almost as good in their season, and far more reliable. These comprise, for succession, St Everard, St Edmund's Russet, Ellison's Orange, Allington Pippin and Laxton's Superb, to name only five of the best and most fertile.

Some of the finest exhibition varieties of cooking Apples are certainly not easy subjects on all soils, and where difficult varieties such as Stirling Castle, Rev. W. Wilks, Gascoigne's Scarlet, Bismarck etc do not succeed, varieties of much the same size and usefulness may be found in the same order in Grenadier, Charles Eyre, Herring's Pippin, The Queen and Arthur Turner, while the qualities of Newton Wonder and Bramley's Seedling are too well-known to need inclusion in this list.

14th September

Recent Rains and High Winds were a reminder that stakes and ties on young trees are frequently in need of renewal or adjustment, and this important matter should be attended to before the autumnal gales arrive.

Dahlias Although the date at which the first killing frost of autumn may be expected varies in different districts – and here in the south Dahlias often continue flowering until November – it is prudent now to go through the whole collection and see that each plant is correctly and legibly labelled. They will all look alike after 8° of frost.

Violets Where these are grown for transplanting into pits or frames for winter flowering, the sooner they are settled in their winter quarters the better. Pits or frames used for Cucumber or Melon crops will be falling vacant at this time. If they have been grown on a leafy hotbed, the whole of the contents, soil and hotbed together, when passed through a coarse sieve will make an ideal compost in which to plant the Violets. Deep pits may be filled to within eighteen inches of the glass with freshly cut spruce boughs for drainage, over which the rougher portions of the compost may be spread and the whole made firm. About six inches of compost will be ample for the Violet roots, which should be lifted from the ground with a good ball of soil adhering. The plants should be well watered in and the lights put on the frames for a few days until the plants have made new roots in the fresh soil, after which the lights may be removed and kept off until frost or heavy rain make it advisable to give them protection.

21st September

Lawns This is a very suitable time for sowing new lawns, and even until mid-October in favourable seasons grass seeds may be sown with every prospect of forming a good green sward before winter sets in. The seeds should be distributed evenly by broadcasting them in two directions, and afterwards lightly raked in and finished off with a light roller.

30th September

Root-pruning Young trees of the stone fruits, such as Plum or Peach, growing in the restricted area against a garden wall are often inclined to make over-vigorous growth at the expense of fruitfulness. To correct this tendency it is necessary to lift and root-prune healthy young trees about every second year, until regular cropping promotes more balanced growth. If this is done at present, while the foliage is still green, and the leaves maintained afterwards on the trees by frequent syringing with clear water, the prospect of a crop next year will be unimpaired.

Older Peach trees also, which have become unhealthy and have foliage of a yellow tint, may often be given a new lease of life by lifting and replanting. This unhealthy condition is often caused through the roots' having penetrated the subsoil, and bringing the roots up near the surface again, with the addition of some fresh soil to which a little bone-meal has been added, will often effect a complete rejuvenation.

7th October

Preparations For Planting Given suitable weather, November is the best time for planting hardy fruit trees, and preparation of the ground should be taken in hand now so that the soil may have a few weeks to settle down after it has been moved. On our clay soil we find it best, when making a new border for wall trees, to take out a trench at the foot of the wall, three feet wide and eighteen inches deep. Good drainage is essential, and this is provided by a row of three-inch drain pipes laid along the bottom of the trench. A four-inch layer of broken bricks is then laid placed in the bottom of the trench, covering the pipes, over which a layer of freshly-cut turves is laid, grass-side down. These turves serve to prevent the fine soil from penetrating into the drainage, and also provide excellent material for the trees to root into later on. Wood ash from the garden bonfire renders heavy soils more friable, and a sprinkling of lime and bone-meal will add fertility. Further organic manure should not be added at planting time, as it tends to the production of rank growth and foliage, instead of the firm, sturdy growth necessary for the production of fruit buds. Soil should be well mixed before filling in the trench, and the whole border made firm by treading.

Such a border at the foot of a wall facing south or west is an ideal site for Peaches, Nectarines or Cherries, a selection of reliable Peaches being Hale's Early, Peregrine, Dymond and Prince of Wales. Four reliable Nectarines for succession will be found in Early Rivers, Lord Napier, Elruge and Pine Apple. When ordering trees of Sweet Cherries – such as Governor Wood, Frogmore Bigarreau, Bigarreau Schrecken and Napoleon – regard must be paid to the fact that all the varieties are self-sterile, and therefore each requires pollen from another variety to fertilise its flowers.

10th October

Sweet Peas Autumn-sown Sweet Peas nearly always give better results than those sown in spring, and the next fortnight is the best time for sowing. The seeds may be sown either singly in two-inch pots, or five in a four-inch pot, with a view to potting them off singly in January. They should be germinated in a cold frame and kept close until the seedlings appear above the ground, after which the frames should be ventilated freely. Sweet Peas are hardy and should never be coddled, but it may be advisable to replace the lights during periods of severe frost or a heavy downfall of snow or rain.

Specimen Plants in Flower Beds Standard plants of Fuchsia, Heliotrope and similar tender subjects are no longer safe outside, and should be carefully taken up and potted and housed for the winter. With careful management such plants will serve to furnish the summer beds for many years. In February they may be pruned and cleaned of dead leaves before starting them into growth again in a house with an intermediate temperature and moist conditions, such as the newly started vinery or peach house.

The beds of summer flowers – now somewhat dishevelled – must be cleared and replaced with plants and bulbs for spring.

14th October

Fruit Picking and Storing All except the very latest-keeping Apples and Pears are now ready for gathering, the exceptions being such long-keeping Apples as Sturmer Pippin and Allen's Everlasting, which must be allowed to hang on the trees as long as possible. If gathered too soon they will shrivel instead of remaining plump and sound until next May or June. This is also applicable to late-keeping Pears, such as Santa Claus, Josephine de Malines, Bergamotte d'Esperen and Easter Beurré.

These latest varieties should be stored at, or near, ground level in the fruit store, several layers deep, to prevent evaporation, but great care should be exercised not to include any damaged fruit, for one decaying fruit will affect all its immediate neighbours. Many apparently sound mid-season Apples have developed various types of decay early in store this season, often due to minute punctures by wasps before gathering.

Hardy Biennials Canterbury Bells, Sweet Williams, Foxgloves and many other hardy biennials should be planted now. The soil is still warm enough to encourage quick rooting, and they should be well established before really cold weather comes. Very pleasing colour combinations are possible nowadays with Canterbury Bells, with their soft-toned pinks and mauves; while the modern Sweet Williams lend themselves to arresting effects when planted in intermingling blocks of salmon-pink, dark crimson and scarlet.

24th October

The Weather The welcome change to drier conditions during the first fortnight of October was most opportune, for although the sudden drop in temperature was decidedly uncomfortable, and frost brought the Dahlias to an early end, nevertheless the fine dry spell afforded ideal conditions for such urgent tasks as the planting of Carnations, biennials and bulbs, and enabled the preparation of the ground for herbaceous plants and Roses to go forward unimpeded.

4th November

Muscat Grapes The bunches still hanging on the vines should be examined frequently for faulty berries.

7th November

Fruits of the Shrubbery Like the garden and the orchard, the shrubbery has yielded a bountiful crop of fruits and berries, the only exception being the larger-fruited Crabs, of whose buds the bullfinches took serious toll last April. Unfortunately, the past tense has to be used in referring to some of the most ornamental species because, owing to the depredations of birds, their display was brief. It is difficult to account for this early and persistent clearing at a time when moisture was too plentiful and the wild fruits of the hedgerow abounded. Some large specimens of Viburnum rhytidophyllum, covered with huge clusters of bright red berries, were stripped clean before a single berry changed to black. Of the Pyrus family, two which escaped bud destruction in the spring, and are among the most beautiful of fruiting trees just now, are Pyrus eleyi and P. aldenhamensis. Their astringent fruits, red to the core, seem distasteful to the birds, but they provide a feast for the eye. The neat orange-red fruits of P. sargentii, on the contrary, were no sooner ripe than they were devoured. The same fate has befallen the plentiful crop on two large bushes of Lonicera maackii and L. hemsleyanum, which last year were thickly studded with bright red berries long after their leaves had fallen. This year, alas! the fruits have gone first. Different species of Cotoneaster vary widely in their attraction as food for birds.

C. franchetii seems to be first favourite, followed closely – and most unfortunately, as it is one of the most beautiful – by C. salicifolia.

18th November

Morello Cherries Walls facing north are often used for this fruit, and in such an aspect lack of sunshine often results in the surface soil becoming sour. Top soil in this condition should be removed down to the uppermost roots and replaced with fresh compost.

Although trees of the Morello Cherry often continue to bear profitable crops when quite old, a time inevitably arrives when, owing to loss of branches or deterioration in size of the fruits, it becomes advisable to grub up and replace with a younger tree. One or two young trees should be kept trained on an outside wall or fence, so that, when a veteran dies, valuable years are not lost before the wall space is again covered with fruiting wood.

23rd November

Fallen Leaves A sprinkling of fallen leaves on the lawn is a natural feature of autumn and not unpicturesque. Heavy accumulations, however, are harmful to lawn grasses, and should be removed. Moreover, the brushing with birch brooms is of distinct benefit to the grass, helping to aerate the soil, besides pulverising and spreading the wormcasts. Fallen leaves should not, however, be removed from shrubberies, for here they form the best fertilising agent. They may be forked in around the shrubs or covered with a layer of fine soil, forming a mulch which will prove of great benefit. Fallen leaves should be removed at once from the rock or alpine garden, except perhaps among the dying foliage of deciduous Primulas.

In the wild or bog garden the leaves of the Gunneras have been blackened by frost, and may now be cut off and placed over the crowns as a protection. In colder districts, dried bracken, or a good covering of tree leaves, packed around and finished off with a few green spruce boughs, makes a safe and not unsightly additional protection.

2nd December

Wiring of Walls The old-fashioned practice of securing branches of wall fruit trees by means of nails or shreds has little to commend it. On the contrary, this ruins the walls in time, while the old nail-holes make ideal nesting-places for injurious insects. In gardens where this old method has prevailed, the changeover to wired walls may be spread over a term of years by taking in hand one wall each winter. The cost of wiring will soon be repaid by the saving of time and cost of nails, while the additional ease with which summer work on the trees can be carried out will be greatly appreciated.

9th December

Pruning With a view to having all wall trees of Plums and Cherries ready for spraying at the end of December, pruning and training should be carried out now. All old ties should be removed and burnt, and replaced with new ties of tarred twine, of varying thicknesses, according to the size of the branches; bearing in mind that large branches become very heavy as the fruits swell, when a tie of inadequate strength may mean loss of a valuable branch through breakage.

On espalier trees of Apple and Pear, all lateral growths should be pruned back to two or three eyes, and each leading growth shortened to about half its length, cutting to a wood bud on the under side.

Although pruning of rare shrubs of less robust growth should usually be practised according to their flowering time and habit, this is not always practicable with large areas of the more vigorous kinds. These may be attended to now during the quiet season, and, in the case of evergreens, the prunings will come in useful for decoration at Christmastime.

16th December

Spraying Cherries, both the sweet and Morello varieties, may be sprayed with a tar-oil wash from mid-December to mid-January, the latter fortnight of this period being suitable also for Peaches, Plums and Damsons. Of Apples and Pears the latter should take precedence, as they usually show earlier signs of bud activity, and both should generally be sprayed before mid-February; but in a backward season Apples may be safely treated as long as the bud-scales have not begun to part.

A still day should be chosen for the work, when there is a prospect of fine weather for at least twelve hours after spraying is finished. In this respect the "wireless" weather forecasts have proved valuable.

19th December

Newly-planted Conifers may need a protecting windbreak, especially where they are exposed to the north or east. Wattle hurdles serve this purpose admirably, or the young trees may be enclosed in a ring of stakes and wire-netting to which garden mats may be secured.

Green spruce boughs tied to a ring of wire-netting probably form the best shelter, however, because they shed their needles gradually in early spring, divesting the young tree of its winter cover as this becomes no longer necessary.

Mid-Winter Work The annual task of tidying up after leaf-fall being now completed, full attention in the flower garden can be given to preparations for the coming year. Alterations in the lay-out of pleasure grounds and flower beds should receive first attention, so that they may be completed before the end of February, after which routine work tends to absorb all available labour. During dry open spells, all hands should be employed on ground work, digging and trenching beds for summer flowers, and clearing up arrears of tree and shrub planting. Driven under cover by rain or snow, there is still plenty of occupation; flower stakes must be cleaned and repointed, and new ones prepared. Labels for all new shrubs and trees may be written and wired, and corms or tubers of Gladiolus and Dahlia, and other dormant plants in store, may be cleaned and sorted.

23rd December

The Christmas Dessert Although imported fruits predominate in markets and shops during the festive season, those more fortunate people who grow their own fruits have ample variety to choose from.

Of the many varieties of Apples, Cox's Orange Pippin comes first to mind. Its season may be a month earlier, but its quality justifies a little extra care in storing so as to have, at any rate, a few in good condition for Christmas Day. A real Christmas Apple is found in Blenheim Pippin, which is now at its best, the smaller fruits being eminently suitable for dessert, while the large specimens provide what is probably the best Apple for mincemeat.

Cockle's Pippin is another old Christmas favourite, its russet and green presenting a foil to the more garish colours, while its distinctive flavour, especially after a sunny season, is much appreciated.

Other first-class dessert Apples now in season are Orleans Reinette, Ribston Pippin, Christmas Pearmain and Laxton' s Superb. The children must not be forgotten, and in the nursery the rosy-cheeked Gascoine's Scarlet and Paroquet are often preferred to more sober-tinted Apples.

That fine Pear Josephine de Malines is usually at its best here at this season, while further north and east its season is much later. The aptly-named Santa Claus is also at its best; and other large Pears now ready are Le Lectier, Nouvelle Fulvie and Glou

Morceau. The smaller Winter Nelis, Blickling, Knight's Monarch and Bergamotte d'Esperen, too, are of excellent flavour.

In a year of plenty, Walnuts and Chestnuts of native origin should be available, and no Christmas dessert is complete without Medlars; their piquant, slightly acid flavour being most refreshing to the jaded palate cloyed with a surfeit of sweets. The largest variety is the Dutch, but the Nottingham Medlar, although small, is of fine flavour. These should have been allowed to hang on the trees until November, and afterwards ripened slowly in a cool fruit room.

II

In the Woods

1930-1934

Ruth Tomalin

October 1930

Walking through the woods one Sunday I came across a dormouse's nest in a bramble clump. I carried it home (to keep it for the winter) and put it in a cage, to find to my dismay that it contained not only a full-grown dormouse but four new-born babies. However, I put some hay in the cage, and for some days fed the mother with nut-kernels and seeds. But soon her attempts to gnaw herself free overcame me, and I took the cage into the woods and there hid it under the bramble clump and opened it.

Next day I found that the mother had made a second nest in the brambles, but the babies were still in the open cage. There they remained for three days, and she fed them.

Then a bad knee kept me at home for four days; when I went again I found that she had taken the hay from the cage and woven it into her new nest; and the babies also had been placed in the nest.

29th November

This morning in the woods I saw a red squirrel burrowing under a tree – apparently for a nut he had buried. Suddenly an owl set up the alarm, and the squirrel bounded away, turning right and left like a lunatic. Then he bounded up a small fir-tree, and I found it held a squirrel's nest at the top, so I suppose he went in there. His fur had a distinct orangey tint.

19th December

Today a boy gave me the foot and claws of an owl. There are four claws, three pointing down and one up, very stiff and sharp.

1st January

First evening owl-hoot (tawny owl) 4.15.

Watched a very little rabbit feeding under a hawthorn. I was about 30 yards off, but a very slight sound from me sent him hopping into his burrow.

2nd January

A new bird came to take food from the sill. It had a black cap, white cheeks, and a brownish-yellow body, and was sparrow-sized. (Coal tit?)

4th January

A nuthatch tapped a cedar loudly for grubs. He had a steely-blue back, red breast and black and white head. In the woods I saw once more the little black, white and red winged bird which, winter after winter, I see and cannot name. It is very plump, graceful and pretty. (Waxwing?)

The Barn Owl flew over this afternoon.

6th January

This morning early I saw a green woodpecker on the lawn, in green jacket and bright red cap, busily eating ants.

7th January

Almond trees have tiny brown, white and pink-speckled buds, like the wings of the Peach-blossom moth.

At dusk the shepherd led home his 200 sheep, himself in front of the flock and the sheep following.

12th January

The Barn Owl was flying towards the keeper's house, and, not wanting him to be shot, I headed him off. He sat on the fence and gravely regarded me.

Sharp frost, but warm sunshine brought several squirrels out. First evening owl-hoot, 4.50.

20th January

Larks singing, and a yellowhammer. One or two bees ventured from their hive in the sun. A red squirrel ran into a fir copse. Saw a brown mouse burrowing in dead leaves.

28th January

Pied wagtail ventured many times into the house for food, and perched on the kitchen table.

31st January

This morning a stoat chased a rabbit on the lawn. Both went off like the wind when they saw me. The stoat was a beautiful creature, red and white, with a sinewy snaky body, blue eyes and a satiny coat. First evening owl-hoot, 5.20.

13th February

On a stone in the stream I saw a grey wagtail – it is yellow-breasted and quite uncommon. Yellowhammers haunt the hedges. The females are yellow-breasted with buff jackets, the cocks rich red and yellow.

25th February

The Barn Owl sits in the elms every evening. He would give a long "Whooo-ooo" and follow it up with a little purring trill, as though to attract another owl. Presently one called from the wood, and he flew over there, "Whooo-ing" loudly. He would sit and preen his feathers in between calls.

27th February

The bees emerged from their hive in clusters, and sunned themselves on the ledge outside.

6th March

Sun, wind and blue sky. Bees in willow catkins. Squirrels gambolling. One, in lovely orange fur, ran up a tree and sat perking his tail, scolding and nibbling a fir cone.

12th March

First tortoiseshell and brimstone butterflies. First thrush's nest.

15th March

Bees pulling dead ones and old comb from their hive.

18th March

In Racton Lane I found scented purple, mauve, pink and white violets, and a dead slow-worm. Saw the Barn Owl this afternoon, sitting in a fir-tree.

20th March

Feeding in a meadow in the rain were two lovely big reddish handsome hares. They pricked up their ears as they fed.

22nd March

Saw what I thought was a sparrow taking a dust-bath. Then it struck me as a queer sparrow. As it flew off I saw by the tuft on its head – it was a lark.

Found three thrushes' nests, a wren's and a chaffinch's, half made. The thrush's nest of 12th March now has three eggs.

23rd March

A wren has built a nest from a heap of moss left at the foot of a tree, and is making a bed of feathers.

In the hedge is a dormouse nest with a hole in the side, showing that the dormouse is awake early. In a gorse-bush there is a little mass of lichen which will soon be turned into a nest by a long-tailed tit. Last year there was a long-tailed tit's nest in the same bush.

26th March

First peacock butterfly, and a cabbage white.

In the roots of a fallen pine is a wren's nest of dry leaves: the third year a wren has built there. Found two more thrushes' nests and a blackbird's, all with eggs. The yews are covered with tiny mealy snuff-coloured flowers.

29th March

The long-tailed tit (23rd March) has moulded the lichen into a cup-shape now, like a chaffinch's nest.

31st March

Dormouse's nest in the woods still has an occupant. One 'blackbird's' nest is really a thrush's, with one egg now.

1st April

Long-tailed tit's nest (29th March) now has a roof.

7th April.

Bright, warm and sunny. Two grass snakes sunning under a hedge. They were fat and long, mottled green and grey.

As I passed the long-tailed tit's nest (1st April) I could just glimpse a bright eye and a little beak through the hole – the hen was sitting. Found several blackbirds' and thrushes' nests with eggs, and a wren's nest made of dry fern.

8th April

A thrush's nest contains babies. Parent birds going to and fro with beakfuls of worms.

10th April

First cuckoo this morning. Last year I heard it first on 17th April. Saw brimstone butterfly and queen bumble-bee. Found more blackbirds' and thrushes' nests with eggs, a hedgesparrow's with four eggs and a robin's ready for laying; also an old squirrel's nut-store (or a field mouse's) buried under a hedge.

11th April

First spring walk over the downs. When we reached the river (near Racton) we looked for water-voles, last year we saw several there. Soon I heard a 'cloop' and there was a water-vole. He drifted with the tide and disappeared under a root.

12th April

Dormouse nest in hedge, neatly woven of grasses. A plump yellow dormouse dropped out and scampered off. He had a sleek yellow head and a lovely fuzzy tail.

16th April

The swallows are here – on the same date as last year.

17th April

Cuckoo calling all day. The woods are full of early bluebells, purple orchises, milkmaids, stitchwort, primroses, violets, wild strawberry flowers, yellow wood-spurge. In the meadows, daisies, dandelions, violets, cowslips. I found an orange cowslip, near the place where a few years ago I found a red one.

19th April

Hedgesparrow's nest in the yew hedge, five eggs. In a cleverly hidden nest amongst some rubbish are five baby blackbirds. Robin's nest in a tin: the mother is sitting. A brood of young thrushes in a nest among some coils of wire netting. Mummie and I freed a squirrel from a trap. (One foot was left behind. It ran up a tree and sat in a fork, scolding us and licking its wound.) Disturbed a little tadpole in the garden pool, the first I have ever seen there. He was not far, I think, from the frog stage. He had his four legs and tail, a 'lizardy' face and crinkled skin. His back was greeny-brown, with brown-speckled white undersides and orange speckles on the underside of his tail, and bright eyes. I shall watch his stages to froghood. (But I didn't. It was a newt.)

<u>23rd April</u>

Nightingale singing in the woods. Found a clump of pale <u>pink</u> wild primroses. In a thorn bush is another beautiful long-tailed tit's nest, and a mistle-thrush's in an apple-tree, with downy babies.

A brown grass snake was coiled round a dry thistle stem, sunning himself.

<u>25th April</u>

Six empty dormouse nests in the hedge round Pitt's Copse. Owl's nest with eggs in a hollow tree in the park. Chaffinch's nest in the cricket pavilion with five eggs. I went to see a robin's nest in the wood and it contained five hot eggs – the robin flew off just then. I know so many thrushes' nests that I have lost count.

<u>26th April</u>

Sedgewarblers in the reeds by the pond. In the marsh, cunningly constructed of reeds and grasses to match the surroundings, was a moorhen's nest with seven eggs. In the shrubbery is a greenfinch's ready for laying.

A fine black and yellow hare leapt from under dry tufty grass in the East Park, and bounded away, ears erect.

28th April

The swallows are here – 16th April was a passing flock. Today they are really home. The young blackbirds and thrushes seen on 19th April have flown. When I visited the long-tailed tit's nest (7th April) the mother popped out, and I could see tiny beaks inside.

29th April

Baby hedgesparrows have spotted orange mouths. Robin babies hatched. White, pink-spotted eggs in a wren's nest. Pheasant's nest, ten eggs, in the rockery.

30th April

In the forest is a wide-spreading old crab tree covered with pink blossom. A goldfinch was twittering in its branches. A hare and rabbit fed together in a ride. Heard a cuckoo that had changed its tune.

1st May

Swallows 'twitting' on the wireless aerial. Cuckoos flying over, calling as they go. A pigeon is lining a hole, high up in a horse-chestnut tree, with horse-hair. A chaffinch's nest in a juniper tree has two eggs. In the fir plantation there are, among other nests, a wren's, a chaffinch's with four eggs, and a hedgesparrow's ready for laying; blackbirds' and thrushes' nests with eggs and babies.

2nd May

Often, though a nest is empty one morning, the next morning it contains two eggs: the first laid late in the day, the second early?

Swallows swooping over a marshy meadow: gnats?

<u>3rd May</u>

Swallows building in the henhouse, a pied wagtail in a broken grating at the top of the peachhouse wall. Saw a hawthorn bush covered with white blossom. Robin babies getting their feathers. Some young thrushes have left their nest and are crouching in the grass, their parents even more fussy than before.

<u>4th May</u>

Railway banks are covered with purple vetch, bugle, the first marguerites, and wild strawberry flowers as big as halfpennies.

<u>5th May</u>

More young blackbirds and thrushes fledged.

In the evening the Barn Owl came lumbering over the shrubbery pursued by a crowd of screaming blackbirds and thrushes. When he perched they flew past him bumping him uith their wings. I think he could not see very well as it was still light, and he kept making little feints at his tormentors. When he flew off they pursued him again.

<u>6th May</u>

Masses of cowslips, pale yellow, warm yellow and orange. Found a red one. A boy brought oxlips to school.

<u>7th May</u>

A hare sat up in a field, ears erect. In the woods, another hare crossed a ride in one terrific bound.

Kingcups in the marshes, and I found a moorhen's nest of dry reeds, six eggs.

<u>8th May</u>

Horse chestnuts in full bloom. Some oak leaves are deep brownish-orange. Found another robin's nest, five eggs.

On the cricket field saw a hawk swooping high and low in his efforts to evade a screaming crowd of thrushes which pecked and pursued him.

Baby rabbits everywhere.

9th May

In Racton Lane I saw a dormouse running up and down a bush, eating bramble leaves. Watched a family of mice in the wood. Saw a wren make twenty-one journeys towards building its nest. Found a pigeon's nest with one egg, a wren's with two, a blackbird's, another wren's with eggs, and an empty robin's. Heard turtle-doves.

10th May

Found ten squirrels' nests in fir trees, and a jackdaw's with two eggs in a hole high up in a tree.

11th May

Two blue-tits' nests in apple-tree holes in the Old Garden. One was full of lovely white pink-mottled eggs. At the other I was greeted by a fierce peck and a snake-like storm of hissing.

12th May

Some wrens' nests are of moss, others of dry fern, others of dried leaves; all lined with feathers and horse-hair, thatched with twigs, and built in some compact and cosy corner.

Chaffinch nests made of lichen, with bedding of feathers and horse-hair.

13th May

Owl calling in the daytime, bats squeaking at night. In a hole in a maple tree is a jay's nest with young ones.

<u>14th May</u>
In the fir plantation is a little green mossy nest, a goldfinch's, with four white pink-freckled eggs. Chaffinch's nest in the cricket pavilion (25th April) has babies. Robins and hedgesparrows flown.

<u>15th May</u>
In the old rock-garden I saw what looked like a blackbird's nest fallen from an overhanging tree. I saw a little bird fly out. The nest was round, of dry grass, cunningly woven into the surrounding ivy, and lined with feathers. It contained several rosy-white eggs, very small, with red-brown frecklings. The bird was small and brown, with dull yellowish wings – a wood-warbler?

<u>16th May</u>
When I visited a chaffinch's nest the mother bird was sitting. She did not fly off, though she looked hard at me.

<u>17th May</u>
At Selborne. Glorious green trees in the beech hanger. Lilac and wistaria around the old cottages. Frogs by a brooklet. The Trumpeter: grave in the churchyard.

<u>18th May</u>
In the wood I came across a mother pheasant surrounded by a cheeping brood of speckly yellow tiny chicks. The mother ran to a little distance, and when she called the chicks answered.

Found five different shades of green-winged orchis in the Garden Field – purple, mauve, velvet-red, pink and white.

<u>19th May</u>
Stalked baby rabbits and got near enough to one to watch it munching.

20th May

Cuckoos call incessantly. Two wrens' and a robin's nests have been torn out. Rats?

Bluebells and young curly bracken mixed with bugle and viper's bugloss. Lovely butterflies on the downs – blues, fritillaries, white ones, brimstones and tortoiseshells.

21st May

Heard a nightingale in the woods. Bat hanging on an apricot tree. Saw a golden-crested wren's nest in a high fir. Found a wren's nest with two bumble-bees in it.

22nd May

A swan on the pond has hatched her eggs, for the first time for years. (She usually deserted after sitting in vain for weeks.)

23rd May

In the meadows buttercups and daisies, purple vetches and marguerites, tiny tormentil and red and white campions, cowslips, red and white clover, purple and mauve green-veined orchises, bugle and viper's bugloss, wild strawberry flowers, dandelions and delicate grasses, and veronica, and fairy-flax, are all mixed up charmingly.

24th May

A hive of bees was removed from the garden today, and the bees have come back to the old site in a swarm.

Found a greenfinch's nest with babies. Saw a baby chaffinch guarded by two watchful parents.

26th May

Saw a brown toad in a ditch, a graceful brown snake in a hedge, many grass-mice and baby rabbits. In an aubrieta clump on a wall is a wren's nest with babies, and there are young ones in one bluetit's nest in the orchard (11th May). Blackbird and thrush fledgelings everywhere.

<u>27th May</u>

The walnut leaves are a lovely copper colour. Saw a hornet.

The thrush which warbled on a hedge-top on 14th January sang there again this morning, as he has done every morning this year.

In the juniper tree is a nest with four cheeping young blackbirds. When I looked at them they opened their beaks wide.

<u>28th May</u>

Thunder-storm. Chaffinch and sparrow bathing in puddles. The swan was swimming with her youngsters.

<u>29th May</u>

In the woods a young jay lay dying, probably because he fell from the nest. He pecked fiercely at my fingers. He had a grey head, brown neck, navy-blue wings, black and white tail, greyish-white breast.

<u>30th May</u>

The warbler's nest (15th May) now contains four naked atoms. Robin babies are speckled brown with yellow breasts.

<u>1st June</u>

When I went near the warbler's nest the young ones opened their beaks expectantly.

<u>2nd June</u>

In the evening I saw two chaffinches hopping and calling in great distress round a broken grating in the peachhouse wall (3rd May). Then a cuckoo flew out! There was a nest in the grating, but no eggs in it.

Today a girl showed me three orchises: a fragrant white Butterfly, a purplish-black aptly named little Fly and an Egg, all comparatively rare.

Some years ago I found a butterfly orchis in the woods. I have looked there every year since, but never found another. Now, in that place, there are four.

<u>3rd June</u>

At Goodwood I found, or was shown, a partridge's nest, eleven eggs; a swallow's with two eggs, another with babies; a linnet's nest with two dear little speckled fledgelings; a greenfinch's nest, two goldfinches' and a robin's, all with eggs; a tit's nest in a drain-pipe.

<u>4th June</u>

Saw a flycatcher fly-catching, and another feeding a baby. The 'greenfinch's' nest is a goldfinch's, with three eggs now. In a tree-fork is a mossy nest with three white brown-speckled eggs, a cross between a robin's and a hawfinch's.

<u>7th June 1931</u>

Wet. Earthquake during night.

After a shower the butterfly orchises smelt very fragrant. Twayblade and green-winged orchises are also out, and foxgloves, wild roses and ragged robins. Yellow irises by the pond.

<u>8th June</u>

In a hole in the wall a nest contains lively young tomtits. In an oak tree is the cleverest chaffinch's nest I have ever seen. It is of grey lichen, only just distinguishable from the grey knobs around.

<u>9th June</u>

Climbed up and examined the broken grating where the cuckoo flew out (2nd June). In it was a pied wagtail sitting on five eggs.

A swallow pair is building in the church porch, using soft wet shucks from the beech-buds, out of the gutters.

The wrens in the aubrietias (26th May) have flown, and I saw them in the shrubbery, about a dozen of them, like little brown butterflies. Also fledgeling chaffinches and a family of tomtits.

<u>10th June</u>

The warblers are now full-fledged (15th and 30th May, 1st June): in light fawn coats and whitish waistcoats, with bright eyes, and little yellow circles round their faces.

Today a <u>canary</u> was flying about in the garden, eating groundsel and grass-seed.

Swallow's nest with babies. First wild strawberries.

<u>11th June</u>

The warblers left the nest today, leaving one egg behind, and their parents are fussing round them.

In the rockery is a little leathery-skinned brown toad with very big bright golden eyes, making a strange 'pop-pop' noise. His home is a deep hole in a stone.

We were much amused watching a mother wagtail and her big fluffy baby. She picked up bread and fed him as fast as she could. All the time he kept fluffing his feathers and screaming. When a cock and hen sparrow came for bread, she angrily routed them. (The birds were being fed owing to a drought.)

13th June
The robin/hawfinch's nest (4th June) is a bullfinch's.

14th June
Snake in the orchard. Blackbirds, thrushes and jackdaws stripping ripe cherries there.

15th June
Saw the toad again and he squirted liquid at me from his skin. Building swallows flew over the stream dipping their beaks in the water, apparently to wet the mud in them.

17th June
Poppies in green corn. Foxgloves, ragged robin, honeysuckle, mauve and white orchids (spotted and pyramid) in the woods.

Walking along a road, I was surprised to hear a tremendous outcry of thrushes; next minute a hawk whirled over the hedge with a couple of baby thrushes in its claws and one parent thrush in pursuit, while the other sat in a tree crying plaintively. The hawk took shelter in oak leaves, and, judging by the noise, it seemed that the parent was fighting for its children.

18th June
The chaffinch's nest in the creepers has been torn out and the babies destroyed. In the nest was a caterpillar which the bird must have brought for its young.

Under a beech is the most marvellous scented orchid I have ever seen, with beautiful white bell-flowers (white helleborine).

19th June
Bee orchises in the grass by the lawn. They have a sweet perfume, mauve green-veined petals, black-and-green smooth 'pads,' tiny white hoods and two orange stamens.

20th June

The swallow babies in the shed have three parents apparently! – three are going about together.

The swallow's nest in the church porch (9th June) has eggs. Skinny babies in the wagtail's nest (9th June.)

Goldfinches go about in bands, feasting on the seeds of tall grasses. Hay is being cocked and smells lovely.

21st June

Saw a handsome little red squirrel by a hedgerow oak; I think he was quite young.

The night lasts only a few hours, and the owls which hoot at dusk must have difficulty in finding food in so short a time.

Cuckoo still calling at intervals, sometimes in its clear April voice, sometimes with its June stutter.

22nd June

The baby swallows have flown from the shed (10th and 20th June). Huge wild strawberries on railway banks (4th May).

25th June

Baby wagtails are acquiring black quills. Saw a flycatcher catch a small tortoiseshell butterfly and eat it. Watched a mother blackbird digging worms and giving them to her baby. Thrush's nest with eggs in a pear tree.

27th June

When I passed a thrush's nest with fledgelings, the mother was standing on the nest with her wings over them.

Saw Sam, our cat, watching a mother rabbit and her babies playing near an old burrow which they have reoccupied.

28th June

Lime blossom out, and the bees are busy.

Sam caught one of those baby rabbits. I carried it back to its home, quaking. It was a plump little thing with soft fur, chubby face, bright eyes and small ears and whiskers.

Saw two young rabbits fighting. They hopped over one another, striking with hind legs.

30th June

Two humming-bird hawk moths on the verbena. First white-letter hairstreak. Found a wren's nest and a spotted flycatcher's, both with eggs.

First white admirals in the wood by the pond, and pink centaury. In the reeds a bird was singing with an exquisite liquid warble. I wonder what it was.

This evening as Sam watched the rabbit-hole, a little owl came and sat on a bough and squawked and made dives at him till he ran away.

Five baby swallows sitting on the wireless aerial, while their parents fed them ceaselessly, each in turn.

1st July

Saw a stoat tracking blackbirds, which chek-chekked at him as he approached, then flew a short distance and continued to annoy him.

2nd July

The baby wagtails have flown from the grating (9th and 20th June), and a baby CUCKOO remains. He is half-fledged and very fierce and ready to peck. His plumage is speckled black and white, and he has a gaping orange mouth. The wagtails are feeding him.

3rd July

Saw a brown grass-snake wriggling into its hole under a bramble, and a beautiful fritillary basking on bracken.

4th July

The baby cuckoo is still in the grating. How will he get out? – he is too fat now to squeeze through, though only half-fledged.

Sam wounded a long greeny-brown snake in the grass, tearing at it with his claws.

5th July

Watched a mole digging for worms. When it saw danger it made straight for a hole and vanished within.

Sheets of blue water forgetmenots on the stream, mingled with canary-coloured mimulus. A moorhen swims there and three fluffy black chicks lag behind, catching flies.

Pinkish-mauve and silver mallows are out, also blue scabious, white privet, woodruff and rosebay willow-herb. Cuckoopint berries are green and will soon turn scarlet. Wild roses are over, and the green hips swelling.

6th July

This evening I got a large cage (to save him from cats) with some hay and a tin of water, placed it on the top of the wall near the grating, brought out the baby cuckoo and put him in it. He is very fierce, like a hawk. His feathers are speckled black and white with red mottling. His foster-parents, wagtails and swallows, are very worried, but are feeding him through the bars.

8th July

Released the cuckoo. He flew off into the garden, followed by wagtails and swallows.

9th July

Showery. Found a drunken bumble-bee and put it on a snapdragon flower. Later it was inside the flower, with the 'door' shut.

A privet hawk moth – which I found last August as a fat green caterpillar, and earthed in a pot of soil – has hatched out of its two-inch brown chrysalis into a glorious moth: brown, with brown-and-white overwings delicately marked, a white collar, striped brown and rose-pink underwings, and a 'tiger' body with rose and brown stripes; the antennae are white, gracefully curved. The moth, released from its chrysalis, flapped to strengthen its lovely wings, and walked round, exercising its legs.

10th July

The moth did not fly last night, as I expected, but settled on a twig near the ground, folded its wings and stayed there all today.

Another chrysalis, found last month in the grass, has hatched into a six-spot burnet moth.

11th July

Burnet moth sucking nectar from sweet-williams with its proboscis.

The thrush's nest in the pear tree (25th June) is full of fluffy new-hatched babies. The young swallows are now flying all around; the parents are again nesting in the shed.

A thrush came for crumbs, made a heap of crumbs in the churchyard and sat there feeding a noisy fledgeling.

15th July

Now the hawk moth has disappeared.

When I was digging I found a lizard, a tiny brown-backed orange-breasted-creature.

16th July
In the park I came on some half-grown baby pheasants, and while they flew away their mother ran round me, distracting my attention from them.

18th July
Lady's-tresses in a beechwood below the downs, also purple pyramid orchids, and three brown bird's-nest orchids in a chalk quarry.
The cuckoo calls no longer. Birds silent, but for a 'ticking' wren.

20th July
Saw two blue butterflies, the colour of harebells, a beautiful little copper, many white-letter hairstreaks, and, on the buddleia, peacocks and tortoishells. In the woods: cabbage whites, meadow browns, white admirals, red admirals and a fritillary with black-marked orange wings and greeny-silver underwings.

21st July
Fledgeling thrushes flew from the pear tree nest.

25rd July
Two red squirrels frisked by the wood. At dusk a brown owl, with big round head and beautiful eyes, flew over; and when we called out he dipped straight down out of sight.
A bat has been in the cricket pavilion after moths, and it is strewn with lovely moths' wings. Found the wing of an emerald moth. In the garden today, a comma butterfly, tortoiseshells, peacocks, whites, hairstreaks, blues, a silver-washed fritillary.
A spotted flycatcher sits on the buddleia bough and swoops after them. Baby flycatchers in a nest on the wall nearby. Three swallow fledgelings in the church nest (20th June) with green-blue glossy wings, chocolate bibs, white breasts, very bright eyes.

27th July

The corn is being cut. Barley and oats are pale yellow, wheat russet-brown. Red berries on rowans. Hazel nuts are creamy-white with green and brown tints. Many rabbits and squirrels about in the woods. Under a hedge I came face to face with a wicked-eyed, red-coated, white-breasted weasel, who turned and flashed away into the underbrush, his tail stiff out behind him.

30th July

Found a dormouse lying on the grass in a ride. He kept jumping up to utter little grunts of fear or pain, but he could not run away, he had lost all his strength. Poor little fellow! A few tooth-marked scraps of toadstool near him almost convinced me that he had eaten a poisonous fungus and was dying of it; or he might have been already ill, eating it for a cure? He presently curled up his tail over his nose, as though he were sleeping, and died.

1st August

Blackberry bushes are covered with pink and white blossoms and hard green berries. Green sloes on the blackthorns.

Bumble-bee's nest in the grass. I found a huge stag's-horn beetle on an elm, with 'pincers' like a crab's.

White-letter hairstreaks cluster in great numbers on the heleniums. They have brown overwings and finely mottled brown-grey undersides, with little orange tips and the beautiful white W mark.

3rd August

A thrush brought a snail to crack on bricks in the back yard. Found two mushrooms and another bumble-bee's nest.

6th August

A fallow deer was seen on the lawn one morning. Red squirrels frisking in the woods. On our rockery I saw a long snake with light-brown V-shaped markings.

8th August

Rabbits had made warm dust-baths in patches of sunlight, in which they were lying.

Purple heather in the woods, pink berries on yews, small green acorns on oaks.

9th August

Every autumn a robin sings from a pinnacle over the church porch. The robins have not yet begun to sing, but today one was ticking at the cat from the pinnacle.

12th August

Most of the corn is in. Scarlet poppies in the stubble. Saw a man ploughing the stubble with a crowd of gulls and rooks following.

This evening, when an old pheasant saw someone coming out to feed the tame pigeons on the lawn, he scurried over to get some food.

13th August

A large company of swallows flying about.

24th August

Honeysuckles and big purple sloes in Racton Lane, also campanula, toadflax, harebells, thyme. Foxgloves in the woods again.

In the moss we saw a fluffy sandy dormouse with long tail and bright eyes – he did move quickly.

Many wasps about, and green and brown grasshoppers, and dragonflies.

27th August

In the grass by the lawns are clumps of sweet-scented white lady's-tresses.

Heard a robin singing. Saw a hedgehog curled in a tight ball.

30th August

Ripe blackberries, elderberries, wayfaring berries, hips, haws, acorns and hazel nuts. Black berries on red-leaved dogwood.

The moon shone down on Bosham harbour (seven miles away) and the waters were like a sheet of pure gold. I have never seen this before.

1st September

Dog violets in the woods. Robins sing all day.

I saw a mole burrowing under the moss. He kept still while I stroked his soft furry back with one finger; but when I moved he turned and scuttled back through the half-exposed tunnel he had already made.

2nd September

Butterflies about: a clouded yellow! also a brimstone, painted ladies, commas, whites, blues, skippers, peacocks, red admirals, fritillaries, tortoiseshells, meadow browns; humming-bird hawk moths, dragonflies and grasshoppers.

3rd September

The dryness is killing off many moles. They keep coming up and dying by their runs.

Owls hooting at dusk.

Found orange, red, green, brown and purple toadstools in the woods. Saw a red squirrel evidently storing hazel nuts already – they are ripe enough to eat. Big long-legged hares skipped in the field by Pitt's Copse. Further on, a squirrel emerged from the hazels, his little mouth full of nuts.

5th September

Robin singing on the church pinnacle. Many others about in the garden and grounds.

A tall wayfaring tree is covered with scarlet bunches of berries, and blackthorns packed with sloes, soft and ripe, with plum-coloured skins and powdery-blue bloom.

Limes, beeches and elms are turning yellow.

7th September

Button mushrooms on the lawn every morning, with satiny skins and fresh-pink undersides.

Wild flowers: meadow-sweet, hardheads, campion, deadnettle, white bugle, blue bugle, mimulus, honeysuckle, water forgetmenots, pink heather, harebells, toadflax, buttercups, flowering rushes, bramble flowers, foxgloves, and mallow, both pink and silver (18).

9th September

Saw a water-vole in the roadside stream near Racton: "a brown little face with whiskers ... small neat ears and thick silky hair."* He was quite tame. Another dived and entered a small hole under the bank.

10th September

In the woods I saw a beautiful red squirrel burying a nut in the moss. When he had finished he whisked away into the hazel bushes.

* *The Wind in the Willows*

Saw a grey squirrel in the garden – at least, he was mainly grey, with a frosty-silver bushy tail, but he had a suggestion of red in his coat. He was not shy, but sat and stared at me before bounding up a redwood tree.

13th September

Hundreds of swallows gathered high up in the air, and flew away.

14th September

This morning I heard a squealing and ran to find the cause, and found a poor half-dead rabbit, while a weasel whisked into a bush.

On the lawn another weasel was performing the queerest antics, dashing to and fro, turning somersaults, twisting about. That means rain? – and, as I write at 8.30 p.m., it is pouring.

19th September

Scabious in the meadows, strings of scarlet and yellow bryony berries in the hedgerows, with heart-shaped leaves of pale yellow or green. Lime trees are yellow, beeches gorgeous russet and bronze. More swallows and martins are assembling, but some are nesting still. Many robins fly about and sing.

Thrushes may be heard among the evening calls, chief of which is the pheasants' roosting-call from the forest.

Saw painted ladies, tortoiseshells, commas, skippers. A little fluffy red squirrel, with bright black eyes and feathery tail, gathered nuts in a swaying hazel bush.

23rd September

When a pigeon was being 'drawn,' quantities of hard-shelled beech nuts were found in its crop. I noticed another wild pigeon eating beech nuts today.

Dozens of little white mushrooms on the lawn. Weasel chasing a baby rabbit.

26th September

In a sheltered corner of the copse hedge six frail white wild roses are flowering, and others in bud. A few primroses and dog-violets in the woods.

27th September

Found a pale-tussock moth caterpillar on a hazel bush – a lovely creature, pale green, with silvery tufts on each section, and deep velvety black incisions, and a red 'horn' on its tail-section, curved upwards, and made I think of fine hairs. It had eight pairs of legs, and moved them in pairs; the wee feet were all turned outwards.

3rd October

Many squirrels gathering nuts and eating them. Gathered acorns for my rabbit's winter food, also dozens of mushrooms.

Swallows about home still, and hundreds collecting on telegraph wires in the village.

7th October

In a beech shuck I found a red six-spot ladybird. She knew where the storm couldn't penetrate. A toad came into a greenhouse in search of winter quarters. He had a floppy rough yellow skin, and seemed to have no bones in his body. When touched he blew himself out and said "Pop-pop-pop."

Grey wagtail by the river (13th February) with canary-yellow underside, black and white wings.

Ivy in flower, and the wasps are after the honey.

15th October

Watched a red squirrel gathering turf, forming it into a ball in its mouth, and moulding it into its big breeding-nest, swung at the end of a pine bough. Though he (or probably she) passed within a few yards of me, he showed no more fear than if I had been a bush.

16th October

Made a hide of boughs, thatched with dry bracken, to watch the squirrel and its nest. I shall leave it for a week to accustom the squirrel to it.

22nd October

Pheasants roosting on the hide.

Traced a mole along his run by his underground squeaks. Found a walnut miles from the walnut trees: carried away by a crow?

25th October

Some fish have been put in a stretch of water and this morning I saw a great flock of herons there.

Finches eating seeds in the flowerbeds, partridges feeding in a stubble-field.

Found first winter dormouse-nest in the woods. Also primroses, dog-violets, deadnettle, pimpernel, wild forgetmenot, bugle and moon-daisies. Toadflax, hawkweed and yarrow in the fields.

27th October

First hard frost – 10° – and ice on the pools. The fields were white, the sun shone brightly and the great russet beech forest stretching away in the distance looked glorious. Gathered sweet chestnuts and mushrooms. Conkers, acorns and beechnuts under the trees, and a red squirrel ran up a beech tree and sat scolding me.

Thrushes eating yew berries. Found a dormouse in a little nest of grass.

31st October

In a forest ride, about fifty yards from me, I saw what at first I took to be a fox, till the head moved, revealing a fine set of antlers. It was a fallow deer, lying sunning himself. Presently he got up and trotted off, his little white bobtail looking very like a sheep's.

A gamekeeper has demolished my hide. He thought poachers had made it to catch pheasants.

2nd November

Dormouse in a nest of leaves. He ran out and sat blinking in the sun.

A crab tree, stripped of leaves, is covered with little rosy crab-apples. Wild cherry leaves are bronze-red.

4th November

Two days of high winds have left many trees half-bare.

7th November

Showery, sunny, windy. Squirrels about, and great tits calling. Pine tree catkins plop down on the moss, scattering pollen.

12th November

A family of fledgeling robins have appeared. There are several young, fat and fluffy, whom the parents bring to the bird-table. As soon as ever it is light in the morning, they arrive in full muster.

Green woodpecker feeding on the lawns again (6th January). Small bat fluttering at dusk, and owls calling.

16th November

On the lawns yesterday a plump little partridge was cropping away at the short grass as hard as it could go. It didn't notice me at first, and I got so near that I could have picked it up. Suddenly it looked up and saw me, and got flurried, running in several directions before it took to flight. Today I saw a partridge eating near the same place. When I was within a few yards it saw me and began to turn round in circles, limp, and behave as though it had hurt a leg or wing.

I suppose this behaviour is common to partridges on being startled, or perhaps I saw the same bird each time, with this habit.

21st November

Many trees are leafless. The sunshine shows up the bare purple boughs, and makes the elms a glorious golden colour. Sticky buds on horse chestnuts, red shiny buds on limes; little grey-green hazel catkins have formed. Blackbirds eating privet berries.

Bees out in flowering thyme. Watched squirrels scratching fleas and washing. Mice squeaking in the dead leaves. Found a blue jay's feather and red robin's breast-feather.

28th November

Beautiful sunshine. The elms are now bare. Primroses in the woods, also speedwell and bugle.

29th November

Bitterly cold. Daddy found a little dead goldcrest in the garden. It is olive-green, very small, with striped golden and ashy cap. A robin came into school.

3rd December

Fluffy young moorhens on the pond. Peewits in the marshy

field, their black, green and white feathers glinting in the sun. Red squirrels out; gnats dancing. Moths at night.

7th December

Fiery red sunrise against the bare forest. The grass shone with silver frost. Robins, wagtails, wrens, hedgesparrows, blackbirds and tits feeding on the window-sill.

Three neat grass-woven dormouse nests in the copse hedge.

21st December

As I passed under a lime tree in the East Park I looked up and saw a beautiful white and golden owl sitting blinking at me. He flew off to a cedar in the pleasure ground where he came when they were shooting in the park.

22nd December

Frosty, with sunshine. Woodmen were burning hazel boughs, from which sweet-smelling blue smoke rose. The sun brought out many red squirrels.

Excellent nuts still under the sweet chestnuts.

A hen goldcrest was found dead, like the little cock (29th November.) She is not so bright, having an olive-green cap.

23rd December

At eight in the morning a thrush sang at the window. A holly in a forest clearing is massed with red berries.

24th December

Primroses in flower on a railway bank.

25th December

I saw the owl (21st December) flying at dusk.

27th December

I went to the owl's roost in the lime tree and saw him sitting there fast asleep, sheltered by brushwood.

28th December

Today the owl was swaying gently on his roost as he cleaned his broad golden wings. He regarded me intently through half-closed lids while I stood perfectly still. Later I heard an owl calling in the distance, and he seemed to be answering from his tree.

31st December

The owl flew over at 3.30 p.m.

I put some bits of meat and nuts on the window-sill for the birds. This afternoon as I watched I heard a tiny rustle in the ivy below the sill. Then something brown appeared – I thought it was a wren, but next moment I saw a pair of bright eyes, and on to the sill climbed a field-mouse, chewing vigorously. A robin scared him and he scampered to one side, but came back in a moment. He was a handsome little fellow, with a white underside and glossy brown back. His whiskers were long and silky. He snatched up a nibbled chestnut and scampered down the ivy with it in his mouth. I put out some cheese for him, but the robin ate it.

III

In wartime

1939-1945

Elspeth Tomalin

Note

In 1959 ET read through her diary and added some notes, shown here in square brackets.

Last week of August 1939

Dublin Horse Show. It was the day of the International Jumping Competition for the Aga Khan's Cup. Competitors were led in by the Irish Pipe Band in their saffron kilts, playing each country's national anthem as they came. It was noticeable what a particularly good reception 'God Save the King' got. Some people rather resented Germany's having the Nazi hymn as well as the old German anthem. The English team were good but not good enough, though Major Talbot Ponsonby afterwards got the special award for his grey. The contest was really between France and Germany, and Germany had hard luck. Everyone admired the plucky German officer whose horse fell at the formidable triple gate (just opposite where we sat) and kicked him. He was obviously concussed, and didn't he get a cheer when he rode in the next round with his head bandaged. The points were heavily in Germany's favour almost to the last, when one of their best horses refused at the double bank and so they lost to France.

Next to us on the stand was a young Kerry man who went through the longest set of adjectives one could imagine as he watched each perfect up-and-over: 'Beautiful – magnificent – lovely' – all with the peculiar rise of the Kerry accent. Delightful. I shall always remember that musical sound.

21st August 1939

Visited a Jewish friend in Dublin. There I felt the chill of fear about the war, she spoke so seriously. We went out into the sunny streets to read the posters about the Russo-German pact.

1st September 1939

At Stansted. Tom (T.E. Tomalin) came in from the estate office and said, "Well, it's started." German troops had crossed the Polish frontier.

September – October 1939

The play being rehearsed by the Stansted Players, The Rose Without A Thorn, was cancelled as many of the young men in it were called up; also the four journeymen gardeners living in the bothy. Services House, the children's home evacuated here from Portsmouth, will require the theatre. Waiting to hear news of a mother and two children to be billeted on me, but instead we have two of the orphanage staff occupying the boys' room.

Tony (second son) was called up again after four days back at the office – he had been at Territorial camp. John Woolfries, the head keeper's son, joins the RAF and hopes to train in Canada. Mrs Woolfries was alone with her little girls from 1914 to 1918 while her husband was in the Middle East. She said, "They've only waited for all these boys to grow up – and it all begins again."

In the Chapel at evensong on September 3rd we sang When comes the promised time That war shall be no more. Heart-breaking.

On the day after our return from Ireland the district nurse called to see if I would start my fifty hours' practice to complete the Home Nursing course. Did one hour morning and evening for most of September. The plucky little patient had a diseased bone and misplaced joint, at first in plaster of paris. I heard she recovered completely.

The Athenia was torpedoed and sunk. (Heard later that the artist Winifred Walker lost her collection of paintings of all the flowers and plants in Shakespeare, on their way to America. She had come here several times to take specimens from the garden. The work was done all over again.)

Mr Lloyd from the Post Office lost his son in the Royal Oak. We no longer hear him whistling in the early mornings. Mr Hussey also lost a son. He came to work here in the gardens soon after. His wife, a very reserved woman, had I have heard a strange experience. She saw her son walk up the garden path, but when she spoke he wasn't there.

Nothing heard from Tony for a fortnight, but we knew he was in Kent (with an anti-aircraft battery) as he had rung one of the family. One Saturday afternoon I saw a soldier walking across the Dutch Garden, and he walked in. I had forgotten he would be a soldier in khaki.

Peter Smith training in the RAF. (1942. Killed in an air accident on the eve of his wedding.)

I have bottled sloe gin, to be kept for Victory Day.

Tom is one of the enumerators for the new National Register, visiting scores of houses to deliver and collect forms and issue identity cards. Regaled with much gossip, and some scandal.

'And each slow dusk a drawing-down of blinds.'

Glorious weather. The gardens at their loveliest, with late summer flowerbeds, herbaceous borders and ripe fruit. Probably we shall never see them like this again. [The annual flowerbeds became additional vegetable plots, and one herbaceous border – pale yellow and white – along the yew hedge on the south front was grassed over. Two girls came to work with the older men on food production. The herbaceous borders in the middle walk were restored after the war.]

Miss C. died suddenly. Mrs G. and I under Nurse's directions do last offices. Have had varied experience on the district and got nursing badge.

Marvellous colours in leaves and berries. First meeting of Women's Institutes Produce Guild. I am a group section leader. In Chichester one evening – first experience of driving in the blackout with dimmed lights – couldn't get car to start. A young airman came along and got it going – said he was in the motor business. Have been round the Institutes for the produce guild.

Filled in ration cards! Wonder what it will be like. [From the first day in 1940 until 1954 we got our weekly rations without fail.]

I have fears of parachute invasion, and am laughed at.

As it gets into November and nothing happens in the way of great air raids, we think it is a strange war.

<u>18th November 1939</u>

At the cinema. Mr Churchill speaking, a fine rousing speech. A 'silent' of Hitler mouthing one of his speeches. Hoots of laughter from the children.

<u>25th November 1939</u>

First week of magnetic mines, a devilish device. Plane over Thames.

<u>December 1939</u>

The Queen paid a visit to Stansted. Next morning was frosty and sunny and HM planted an oak tree. She looked lovely – all in black with beautiful pearls and dainty little velvet shoes with such high heels. I felt sorry for her walking across the rough gravel. All the children from Forest Side school and Services House orphanage were there. HM is far prettier than her photographs show, she has wonderful blue eyes and such a sweet smile. We were all surprised she seemed so shy. She spoke to some of the children. The Matron and the Head Teacher were presented, and Mrs Lloyd who lost a son in the <u>Royal Oak</u>.

We heard after that there was jealousy among the Home children as one child HM spoke to had only arrived the day before!

One wonders what Stansted will be like when that oak is full grown. (1989: over 45 feet high).

8th January 1940

Rationing began. Sugar 12 oz, bacon 4 oz, butter 4 oz (later 2 oz) each per week. Meat to be 1/2d worth.

15th January 1940

Three of F's evacuees (at Manor Farm, Walderton) from London had never used knives and forks. They also didn't understand how to use the handle on a teacup – but F. said they were 'Nature's gentlemen', they had such nice ways.

2nd February 1940

Bitter cold weather. Snow – then on Saturday and Sunday rain, which began to freeze, and by Sunday morning all the twigs were two or three times their usual thickness with ice. When the branches swayed in the wind they tinkled and rattled, an eerie sound because it was so unusual. The ground was a sheet of ice. Nobody had ever known it in such a condition. All electric trains stopped. Gerald (elder son) and John Woolfries, here on weekend leave, took five hours to get up to town by steam train on Sunday night. Deep snow on Monday. Began to thaw on Wednesday, but very slowly. Today (Friday) roads still very bad in places under the slush. On Thursday went to a committee meeting for canteen in Westbourne for 300 or 400 men at the camp.

Very bad type of 'flu prevalent with sore throat and temperature. Gerald has to register (for war service) on the 17th. He will try to get into the Royal Artillery.

Meat not yet rationed. Allowed more bacon – double ration.

15th March 1940

Went to London for the first time since war began. From Petersfield it snowed hard all the way. At Waterloo it was very cheerless, crammed with soldiers, all looking so serious. Outside the streets had inches of slush and a blizzard was blowing. Went to WI cookery conference at Queen Mary Hall: rather dull, except for a delegate from Durham. I always find these North Country women have more vitality than South.

April 1940

Norway and Denmark invaded. A few miles nearer to us. Marvellous Naval work: but what a cost!

May Day 1940

Spoke to Tony on the 'phone. Immediately realize he is going abroad. I think of Norway. He had 72 hours' leave. Beautiful weather. It is very sad to think it may be a long time before we are all together again with the boys of the family. [It was Easter 1947.]

10th May 1940

We hear of the invasion of Holland and Belgium. Wonder if Tony will be sent there. At present he and Peter Kershaw are manning a gun in a field. Wonder how long they will be there – but as it is against parachutists I am relieved. This last week a lot of people are wondering about parachutists, and Mr Eden has started the Local Defence Volunteers.

15th May 1940

Drove to Trotton with Tom. Saw Mrs Mullins's garden at the Dower House. Full of treasures, as is the house. Mrs M gave me a Pasque flower and Essex primrose. Lovely day.

22nd May 1940

News very bad. Heard Reynaud's despairing speech. [The gravity of the situation was felt much more than is expressed here – but I would not write it down.] Reading Edna Ferber's autobiography A Peculiar Treasure, and again a Jew makes me afraid. Glorious weather. No news of Tony.

24th May 1940

Very depressing day. Questions in the House about enemy landing in Ireland. No news of Tony. Enemy in Boulogne! Fine speech by the King. What hard tasks he has had to face since coming to the throne. Went for a walk up Racton Lane and in the East Park. Never saw the hawthorn so lovely. (1943. Bushes torn out by bulldozers and a great crop of wheat there.) The blue poppies are out in the tennis court garden, and all the flowering shrubs.

Mary Sykes (19) is a nurse in the London Hospital. The headmistress once called her a flibberty-gibbet: and is there one of the 'scholastic' girls as much use in the world today?

'All day long the noise of battle rolls…'

Heard with relief Tony at Mitcham. Did not know where he was during the terrible news from France. The draft for France stopped just short of them.

25th May 1940

Terrific explosion – said to be magnetic mine off Hayling. News of Belgian capitulation. What will happen to our poor men left there? [News of Dunkirk was not yet widely known: only at points where they were landed.]

29th May 1940

In Chichester at WI Rally. Left me depressed. All these silly women: what will they be like in real trouble? [They were grand.] They were singing 'Run rabbit run' – I hadn't the heart to join in. They are so phlegmatic in South England – yet it is their strength too I suppose.

30th May 1940

Letters in the papers on home defence. Think idea to remove signposts jolly good. [We cursed this afterwards.]

1st June 1940

Heard of the evacuation of the BEF from Flanders. Marvellous gallantry. If only one could do something to help. Driving people to St John Ambulance classes in Chichester – and doing a bit of hoeing. Produce Guild needs to do more towards food.

5th June 1940

Heavy gunfire at night, and flashes in the west. Thinking of invasion. The All Clear – then heard a train – then an owl. These sounds are always so comforting. They seem so sane in a mad world. Glorious weather, clear light. Haying started. Wild roses out. What will have happened before they flower again? It doesn't bear thinking about. No word of Tony.

Butter, bacon, sugar rations 4 oz each per week. Allowing Tom and myself one tablespoonful of sugar each day, kept in different coloured little bowls.

LDV keeping watch against parachute invasion. Have also fear of enemy being landed by gliders.

Lord Duncannon got back last Sunday from Dunkirk – terrible experience, two men with him killed – he only got a splinter. Patrick Baring killed, only 21.

11th-14th June 1940

Italy has declared war on us. The stab in the back. But I don't like some of the things said against Italians – it seems too much like German speeches. Mr Barrett Secundus, a kindly man, said today he hoped the little old organ-grinder would not be interned.

14th June 1940

Paris has been entered. It is very black – but never say die. I expect it will soon be our turn to see them on our soil. We have had wonderful freedom so far in this beautiful June weather – only no rain and the crops are gasping. Spain is rather uneasy: what will they pressure her to do?

17th June 1940

Heard one o'clock France ceased fighting. Knew by his voice what announcer was going to say.

23rd June 1940

In the Chapel we heard: 'Defend us in all assaults of our enemies … defend us from all perils and dangers of this night … because there is none other that fighteth for us …' How many years of history since those words meant so much.

25th June 1940

Air raid warning last night. It always sounds like the hounds of hell. Heard no planes. In Chichester people looked worried – the first time I have noticed this. Guns passing through the streets. Gave a Yorkshire fellow a lift to Funtington. He had been at Dunkirk -very jumpy, poor soul.

[One of our journeymen gardeners, back from Dunkirk, told me about the terrible bombing and machine-gunning along the roads. And he said he hated seeing the tulip fields in Holland smashed up.]

26th June 1940

Air raid warning last night, heard planes circling, but fell asleep. To Funtington today to WI canning school. Everyone seems dazed and wondering what the future holds. Life is like a dark passage with no light beyond. Such lovely weather – though rain does not come. How we should have enjoyed such weather in other days. Thank God for books. So many people lately have quoted Hardy's 'Only a man harrowing clods …'

2nd July 1940

The corn is ripening. WIs to have the work of distributing extra sugar for preserving. On Saturday night bombs dropped on farm in North Marden – terrific bang. Thought it was the AA gun at Sindles. No one killed, mercifully. Nightmare world still goes on.

5th July 1940

Have had some welcome rain. Everyone sowing vegetables. Planted red cabbages in my flowerbed. Soon the harvest will be on. Who will reap it – Englishmen or death? Hope to go to WIs at Sidlesham, Walderton, Marden to talk on drying and storing vegetables. Air raid warning as I set out for Emsworth. At Monk's Hill met a girl with her baby in pram, quite unconcerned. Air raid wardens about, but everything going on as usual – the English are not easily perturbed.

Marden had a second enemy visit – for photography? – in daylight. They got a fright at second swoop. It is such a quiet lonely place in a fold of the downs.

Should not be surprised to hear Ireland occupied. Against us? Wait and see.

12th July 1940

Three enemy planes brought down – unfortunately in town – witnessed by most inhabitants quite wrongly.

Went to Coldwaltham. Tom lectured. Barrages on roads, reminded me of Ireland long ago. This has been declared a restricted area (no visitors) but no restriction if it is your home.

<u>13th July 1940</u>

WI meeting, spoke on vegetables. Air raid warning just as we were leaving. Everyone quite calm.

Church bell-ringing now prohibited except as warning of attack. In …… the bells were heard just after the siren. Vicar and air raid warden went to see what the sexton was up to. He said, "When they sirens went I thought I had to ring them bells." Great fuss, military and police demanding explanations. Everyone thought invasion had started. Back to the Armada.

<u>19th July 1940</u>

WI meeting at Ashling, Tom speaking on second cropping. Planes overhead as we drove – the warning had gone. F's evacuees have gone back to Portsmouth!

Lieutenant-Commander Gordon Smith died this week – hero with Commander Warburton at the battle of Narvik, left for dead and rescued by sailors (got DSO few weeks ago) but had sustained a fractured skull and died after an operation. Deeply sorry for his parents.

Ray in Royal Signals. RS camping here in the Park. It would be an amusing coincidence if he were here. Later – we hear he has gone to India.

<u>5th August 1940</u>

Bank holiday, only in name. Many people have a few hours off, just for a rest. Gerald here, will spend a week harvesting. Tony in Wales.

We are getting used to the ration of 2 oz tea per week. Have coffee for breakfast, so have not had to cut out 'early cup'. Meat is enough and I have a rabbit to help out at weekends. Have made a lot of jam and bottled much fruit. Lovely evening, though marred by sound of gunfire. We should be used to this after fifteen years of Naval testing at Portsmouth.

8th August 1940

Siren this morning. Planes very high, went out with fieldglasses. Saw three and felt sure they were enemy. After lunch heard plane and AA fire – the garden men saw the plane. Yesterday saw a helicoptor flying very low. Today the pilot, Squadron Leader Gilbert Elliott, staying at Stansted House. On nine o'clock news heard of big attacks on convoys. Fifty-three brought down, sixteen of ours missing. At least sixteen homes bereft.

Watched the harvesters making a stack in Mr Gauntlett's enormous wheatfield near Funtington. The precision of the men's placing of each sheaf was like a rhythm. Up and up went the stack, the wagons kept bringing loads, but the field is so large that it had hardly been touched when they had done two stacks. Planes patrolled round and round on their ceaseless watch. As the sun sank I came home on the old bicycle, overhead squadron after squadron of rooks sailing back to the beeches round the little church at Lordington where I suppose they have roosted for generations. The valley was very peaceful. I am reading the history of Bourne (Westbourne) once more* and came down the Packhorse road (Racton Lane).

12th August 1940

Hell let loose. [Air attack on Portsmouth and then the Battle of Britain.] Gerald very thrilled, wished he had joined the RAF. He left for Shoeburyness (RA training station) on Wednesday. Scream of diving bombers and falling planes. One down at French's Farm, three crew dead. Crowds coming to see the wreck. They may see enough before it is all over. Yesterday the noise went on all day, air raid warnings day and night. Glorious hot weather. Perfect holiday weather in other days.

*<u>Bourne In The Past</u> *by J.H. Mee, 1913.*

26th August 1940

On Saturday the gardens were open for the Nursing Association. Heavy daylight air raid on Portsmouth, cinema hit. At night standing at the front door watched the searchlights on a plane – realized that when they got right on to it it would drop its bombs – it did so just as we dived in. They fell in the Rough Avenue.

31st August 1940

Awakened by screaming bombs which we waited to smash us, they seemed so near. Some fell near the cricket field, others at Sindles. Our dear old cat Sam was a casualty.

6th September 1940

Again wakened at 2.30 a.m. by screamers, not so near as the others. Went out to look if any fire. Saw a glow which we guessed was at Walderton. Heard at breakfast time four houses demolished and a granary set on fire. Later, heard no houses damaged and no casualties – only Mrs C's granary.

7th September 1940

Great activity. Wailing Willie [sirens] at 10 p.m., heavy gunfire until about three a.m. Had feeling something more than usual. Bulletins about raid on London.

8th September 1940

National day of prayer. Heavy raid on London, 400 killed, 1400 injured. Unfortunately this is true! Letter from Gerald at Shoeburyness. Heavily bombed. Hope he is moving Tuesday.

9th September 1940

Raids on London continue.

10th September 1940

Two of the gardeners thought they heard church bells. Hector (the foreman) went off on his motor bike to tell Major Bollam, in command of the local Home Guard. A false alarm. Rumours of invasion going round.

Picking blackberries in the East Park. Suddenly out of the clouds appeared very high twelve black planes. Had on white coat so sat on one of the white stones put there by Major Bollam against landing aircraft. Afraid to use fieldglasses as planes looked like enemy. Another twelve appeared, and also very low two of our biplanes. They were all ours.

16th September 1940

Tonight's the night! [Invasion expected.] People at Westbourne canteen not worried about results – nearly all Naval people and great is our faith in the Navy.

17th September 1940

Still here. Heard bomb drop at lunchtime, then the siren. Heard it was Copnor church. 10 p.m. Siren gone – the old drone of planes overhead.

8th October 1940

To Chichester to hear food lectures. Mabel Constanduros (a popular broadcaster) 'babbling on green veg' and Sir Jack Drummond on the more scientific side. Lorries were parked outside Emsworth Lodge. On the way home went in to see Mrs Evans's lovely garden – sirens went. Hurried off, hearing heavy guns. All along the road saw people standing on the fence or with their bicycles, looking towards the west – but didn't stop. At Churcher's Corner saw what looked like two of the Thorney Circus – as we call the Coastal Command planes that patrol so

Issued by the Ministry of Information  *in co-operation with the War Office and the Ministry of Home Security,*

If the INVADER comes

WHAT TO DO — AND HOW TO DO IT

THE Germans threaten to invade Great Britain. If they do so they will be driven out by our Navy, our Army and our Air Force. Yet the ordinary men and women of the civilian population will also have their part to play. Hitler's invasions of Poland, Holland and Belgium were greatly helped by the fact that the civilian population was taken by surprise. They did not know what to do when the moment came. *You must not be taken by surprise.* This leaflet tells you what general line you should take. More detailed instructions will be given you when the danger comes nearer. Meanwhile, read these instructions carefully and be prepared to carry them out.

I

When Holland and Belgium were invaded, the civilian population fled from their homes. They crowded on the roads, in cars, in carts, on bicycles and on foot, and so helped the enemy by preventing their own armies from advancing against the invaders. You must not allow that to happen here. Your first rule, therefore, is :—

(1) IF THE GERMANS COME, BY PARACHUTE, AEROPLANE OR SHIP, YOU MUST REMAIN WHERE YOU ARE. THE ORDER IS "STAY PUT".

If the Commander in Chief decides that the place where you live must be evacuated, he will tell you when and how to leave. Until you receive such orders you must remain where you are. If you run away, you will be exposed to far greater danger because you will be machine-gunned from the air as were civilians in Holland and Belgium, and you will also block the roads by which our own armies will advance to turn the Germans out.

II

There is another method which the Germans adopt in their invasion. They make use of the civilian population in order to create confusion and panic. They spread false rumours and issue false instructions. In order to prevent this, you should obey the second rule, which is as follows :—

(2) DO NOT BELIEVE RUMOURS AND DO NOT SPREAD THEM. WHEN YOU RECEIVE AN ORDER, MAKE QUITE SURE THAT IT IS A TRUE ORDER AND NOT A FAKED ORDER. MOST OF YOU KNOW YOUR POLICEMEN AND YOUR A.R.P. WARDENS BY SIGHT, YOU CAN TRUST THEM. IF YOU KEEP YOUR HEADS, YOU CAN ALSO TELL WHETHER A MILITARY OFFICER IS REALLY BRITISH OR ONLY PRETENDING TO BE SO. IF IN DOUBT ASK THE POLICEMAN OR THE A.R.P. WARDEN. USE YOUR COMMON SENSE.

constantly – flying away from each other, not together as usual. The lorries were still parked, so as it was dusk had to go rather slowly up the hill to the Emsworth Lodge. About halfway along the drive to our white gate there was a tremendous roar and through the elms began to appear a light. Instantly realized it was a burning plane. It came down 100 yards away in front of the white gate, and all behind it was a sea of flames. At the same time overhead roared a plane firing its machine guns, and two planes marked with crosses passed low in front of the car and the burning plane. I just got the impression through the windscreen of these planes zigzagging and firing terribly, but I looked more at the burning plane, I did not realize the danger. All the time there was the crackle of bullets from the burning plane and the coloured flames of incendiary bombs. I started to back the car – turned it on to the grass and drew up under the oak trees (why, I wonder) about 200 yards from the plane. Got out and heard heavy firing. Actually this was bombs being dropped in the drive near Middle Lodge. Noticed flames high up behind the elms and thought the bothy was on fire and thought of the nurses and babies staying there from Services House. Got back into the car, and just then there was another terrific roar, and through the window I saw a mushroom of flame and smoke going up from the crashed plane and I think the car rocked a little. Three carthorses galloped past snorting. Black bits of debris were flying in the light of the fire. Till then I had not once thought of bombs.

I started the car and went back on to the drive. As I reached it a young soldier came up on a motor bike and gasped "Are you all right?" Two more soldiers called to him in the dusk and he went off. A young officer rode up and said I could go round by the road. All this time in my mind I thought all these incidents were connected and it must be invasion. Actually all three were separate – the presence of the soldiers, the fall of the burning plane and the battle between fighters overhead. I got to the Emsworth Lodge again and told a group of soldiers a plane was down. Mr Gale (gamekeeper) heard, got his Home Guard armlet and rushed off. (The Home Guard stood guard by the wreckage until the Army took over.) Neither these soldiers nor those in the park believed there was a plane down. They thought it was just dropped bombs. I assured them I saw the plane come down. They had greeted me by shouting "Put those lights out!" – I don't think I had realized I had the car lights on. I drove round by Middle Lodge in what was by now almost darkness and got to Stansted House, where Lady Moyra told me all the windows were gone, and pointed to the blinds torn to shreds. It was only then that I realized how great had been the explosion. I walked on down to the gardens. It was too dark to see that the Chapel windows too were gone, but I saw a big lump of stone on the ground. Then it occurred to me to wonder if anything had happened to our house.

It had. As I came round the yew tree by the Chapel I saw gaping holes where the windows had been, all the woodwork of the frames smashed and hanging out, and the curtains caught up on them. I opened the front door to find Matron and Miss Bailey inside and several excited small children, half undressed, sitting on the stairs. They had been getting ready for bed when the burning plane came over. The first roar I had heard must have been the explosion of the petrol tank, somewhere about the large macrocarpa tree in the pleasure ground. The plane crashed through that, stripping the boughs from the middle and leaving a long stem with boughs at the top, just like a Christmas tree. Matron was in their quarters in Stansted House, and at once set out to run down to the children in the bothy, her little dog following. Both were blown into the shrubbery by the bomb blast, and she found herself lying on the ground. She thought the terrible noise would never stop, then they got up and ran on, finding the bothy empty and the occupants in our house fifty yards away. The bothy windows were smashed by that first explosion, and when the plane crashed close by Miss Bailey rushed the children over into our hall: our front door is heavy old oak, probably once part of the Chapel.

Everyone had wonderful escapes, all except poor Mr Elliott, the young airman staying at Stansted House, who ran down towards the plane thinking it might be one of ours. He was injured by flying debris and died two days after. Such a sad waste of a fine young life. He said he saw four men in the plane before the bombs went off.

Tom was all right. He had been crossing the south lawn and threw himself flat when the bombs exploded. All the rooms in our house except two were a mass of glass and wreckage, the kitchen full of plaster and soot, the kitchen window gone but not the skylight. A huge bowl of vegetables, being salted down for pickling, was thick with powdered glass. The yard, garden, pleasure ground and frameyard were strewn with broken glass, slates and debris from the plane and the greenhouses, smashed by the petrol tank explosion. An unexploded bomb was found near the wreckage, and bodies. It was guarded and we slept on mattresses in a room at the back of the house [the only time we did this all through the war.] Next day the bomb was removed by the Army. Human remains and debris had been flung far and wide – a huge part of the plane engine was near Middle Lodge.

The German fighter plane is believed to have been one that machine-gunned Havant and Emsworth – that was what people were looking at on the way home from Chichester. Also that evening people in Walderton and Forest Side were knocked over by the blast of the bombs going up, yet I – so near in the car – felt hardly anything, and the three horses were untouched. We would appear to have been in a segment of a circle scarcely touched by the blast, and had a most amazing escape.

[About ten years after, a boy prowling about found a German wrist watch in good condition, and he kept and wore it.]

So much for our bomb story.

<u>27th October 1940</u>

Awakened at twenty to seven by the explosion of three bombs in the warren. I heard a plane as if it had gone mad – nothing fired at it. We heard after that it was brought down by guns off the Isle of Wight.

<u>14th November 1940</u>

This evening at sunset a huge white moon was rising, turning the dead bracken in the East Park to copper colour. Barn owls and tawny owls flew about calling loudly and answering one another. The tulip tree in the pleasure ground was bright gold in the dusk and the young blue cedars silvery. Then before dark we heard planes – the sirens and the guns started up together.

<u>15th November 1940</u>

A terrible night. The noise was ceaseless, the guns going and planes streaming over hour after hour in brilliant moonlight, apparently going due north. Then coming back again, some sounding very strange as though about to crash. We could only listen and think – some poor souls are getting it. Today we hear it was Coventry.

<u>30th April 1941</u>

November – April, food not so plentiful, but lots of vegetables, oatmeal, flour. Keep sack of oatmeal in and feel it a good standby. During the raids I cook our supper by candlelight on an oil stove in the scullery (not sure of skylight blackout) – e.g. home-grown haricot beans, home-made tomato sauce, a scrap of bacon. Eggs now more plentiful, cheese rationed May 1st.

In November Tony drove from quiet Wales into a bad London blitz.

Going to the Orkneys. Gerald at OCTU at Catterick. Ruth in the land army at Brinkmans' fruit-tree nurseries at Bosham. Very sorry to hear that my cousin Willie Mitchell went down in the Rajputana.

Portsmouth had a land mine raid just before Christmas and many more bad raids in the new year. Emsworth Square all glass and roofs gone, a mine in the mud near the harbour. This was when we hoaxed Jerry with decoy fires. Many people out from Portsmouth at night, two sleeping at Middle Lodge and four at Drew's Farm. It is pitiful to see the trek out each evening. I have a mother and two boys from Services House. Tom and I fire-watching each Saturday night in Stansted House. There is a rota and we all do a turn. We sit in the library and when an Alert is on we put out lights and open the south and west windows. Watch the stars travel across the sky and can almost tell the time by them now. Saw two falling stars. Had incendiaries dropped all round one Sunday night in March. Hector put them out. Two exploded. None fell on buildings. An order some time after this forbade going near them if not on a building. Christmas 1940 we spent alone, sad after the jolly times.

Pheasant and plum pudding for dinner. In February some of the family from Kent came for a weekend – Louise said it was a 'delayed action' Christmas.

I am on West Sussex WI executive council. At a cooking and dietetic conference in Chichester Dr Drummond spoke on vitamin values of vegetables, milk and brown bread, exploding the idea that one needs white bread and meat.

In April: overheard at a WI conference in Chichester, held in the old ballroom of the Dolphin Hotel. The All Clear was sounding and an earnest delegate enquired, "And does that mean that it's all over?" I expect she came from a country district where the sirens aren't heard. Coming home saw two little nippers getting over a stile: "Is this the way for the bombs please miss?"

Today my Portsmouth evacuee Mrs Owens described the terror of being in a shelter in Portsmouth with her children from 9 p.m. until 4.30 a.m. while the bombs screamed down and land mines did terrible damage – then she added, "But we're not so bad as Plymouth." The kindliness of people! And she had lost all she possessed except her children.

May 1941

The battle for Crete. Dress rehearsal for invasion here?

20th June 1941

Mrs Riggs, Music, WI Headquarters, told us of a small Institute in Berkshire which had been bombed, lost all its windows and was also looted of all its possessions. They sang so well she congratulated them. One member got up and said, "Yes, we'll sing. That Hitler would like to stop us, but he won't." That's the spirit.

3rd August 1941

Lord Bessborough was scything the cricket field for hay with Mr Chase (stableman and beekeeper). When Chase came down this evening he remarked, "My mate's still at it."

16th August 1941

Today we visited Southampton. Tom was judging at a show and fete. It was a lovely day of high white clouds in a washed blue sky after heavy rain yesterday. We found the County Cricket Ground easily [no signposts]. I must tell Tony the sacred pitch was roped off for safety. The scoreboard still had the numbers up – Last man 8 – wickets 3. It all looked very forlorn and like something left over from another world, which it was. The promoters of the show had decorated and brought some semblance of gaiety to their part of the grounds. Down the High Street there is terrible destruction – blocks still standing here and there, an occasional shop open, acres of desolation in between. I walked through scenes like those in 'Things To Come' (film by H.G. Wells) – prophetic phrase. The Bargate stands solidly across the street, apparently untouched, and the walls on the dockside, also the famous Tudor House, and a church near with a graceful spire. It is really a deserted city – so many houses are empty. There were no boats in, and all the cranes standing up straight, and grass growing at the sides. Few people or traffic passed along the dock road. Very different from my former visit about ten years ago to see the Empress of Britain, white beauty now alas! at the bottom of the sea. But the Common in the centre of the city was ablaze with flowers.

23rd August 1941

Weather very unsettled, bad for the harvest. Gardens opened on Saturday and it poured all day – two people came. Sunday was a nice day – over 70 visitors.

Had for lunch delicious rabbit pie (rabbit 1s), steamed marrow, new potatoes, fruit in jelly. Not bad for wartime. Am bottling fruit and tomatoes, and pulping apples.

28th September 1941

Have had a week's rest. Lovely weather. Drove to Aylesbury, stayed at the Bull's Head and Bell, went to Latimer, Waddesdon and Oxford, came home by West Wycombe, Henley and Alton. Very difficult to find the way, as no signposts and people very reluctant to give directions! We had saved enough petrol to take us to Aylesbury and back, but had to use bus or train for our expeditions.

Bushy mimulus growing on the banks of the Thames. Oxford's beauty in stone – the lovely quadrangles and their turf – the old mulberry trees and the green of the Meadows seen from Magdalen Bridge. No traffic on roads nowadays. Miles without meeting anything but a lorry.

John gone to the Middle East. Ray in Irak. Gerald has left Catterick, September 19th.

Food very good while on holiday – rather a lot of fish. Eggs now rationed to three a month, sugar 8 oz, cheese 3 oz a week, (agricultural ration 8 oz), meat 1/2d worth, butter 4 oz, bacon 4 oz. Food situation wonderful really. There has been a shortage of oatmeal, but better now.

19th February 1942

Quiet nights. Christmas very quiet. Had pheasants and Christmas pudding, Tom whiskey – no wine! Hard weather in January and continuing until now. Gerald had embarkation leave. Mrs Wilder (92) buried today in the churchyard in her husband's grave: he died in 1896. What a short time it takes to get rid of one! Service only a few minutes. Bitterly cold. Very depressed.

On Friday the 13th we heard of the escape of German vessels from Brest – but we're not beaten yet. Great deeds of Esmond and his companions, another Irish VC.

27th March 1942

Glasgow Orpheus Choir broadcast. 'Where Hope dwells … It's aye summer there.' Soloist Jean Houston.

Had a letter from Gerald written on St Patrick's Day – evidently he was going next day, though he didn't say. Lovely spring weather after very cold winter. Planes very busy day and night, we guess going out on raids. Tony on leave from Orkney. He brought butter, eggs and his chocolate ration which he had saved.

April 1942

Was in London. Few people about and little traffic. Saw a horse cab! WI annual Council meeting at County Hall, Chichester. Am again on executive committee. Had lunch at Kimbells, 2s – soup, ham and tongue, salad and potatoes, rhubarb and custard or apricot sweet. British Restaurant opened a week ago, not very good yet.

25th April 1942

Letter from Gerald evidently from a port – Lagos? Fire-watching. Two Alerts and heavy gunfire. Bath, Exeter, Norwich, York on successive nights – 'reprisals.'

7th August 1942

Have just put four children's Empire Day medals in salvage, and ribbons in ragbag.

January 1943

In London for WI food preservation meeting. Asked to be steward at AGM in June, if held. Lord Woolton spoke and was quoted on the wireless.

14th February 1943

Went to Chichester shopping. Decided to go back by 4.07 train and not have tea. As we drew out of the station the Alert sounded – as the train went along I felt something was happening. Told at Emsworth that a bomb had been dropped at Havant and two planes had flown along the line machine-gunning, though we heard nothing in the train. Bombs at Chichester doing heavy damage to life and property – one in North Street almost next door to Kimbells, so I was lucky not to have gone there to tea. Tom was giving a talk at Walderton WI and said planes passed low over the car at Aldsworth bridge, machine-gunning.

We are spellbound by wonderful Russian success – wonder if they will stay at frontiers. Tom reminded me of G.B.Shaw's letter in the Times and scorn poured on it.

Spring very early this year. Snowdrops out soon after Christmas, and catkins. Gathered violets in the old orchard today. Gales have brought down a lot of wood. Yesterday did some gardening as it was dry. Ground not fit to touch since November.

Tony on leave, glad to have a few extras for him, pheasant got just before the end of the season and kept in hope of his coming.

The planes are going out. How thankful we are that they are not now coming in in the same fashion. Women everywhere always say, "We must not grumble, we are well off." Hear of starving children in Europe, enough to break any woman's heart. Can we help – or will it be too late? The speaker described them in Greece as Compton Mackenzie did. It is terrible to sit and only be able to look on.

6th April 1943

A lovely spring afternoon with the shiny new leaves on the beech trees just showing a haze of green. Met a small boy on Forest Side hill wandering down from school by himself, obviously enjoying life. He greeted me with, "Isn't it a nice day?" He was right, it was a gem-like day.

This evening, picking rabbits' food in the orchard, I heard the far-off roar of fighters. They came over the East Park, just skimming the treetops: 2-5-7, then 8-9-10, and after a long interval I counted 11: where was the 12th? We have got the habit of counting them in and out. They fly with a roar just over one's head, usually in sixes or twelves. Whatever I am doing, when I hear them I feel I must drop it and go to look at them and pray that they will come safely back.

Still fire-watching on alternate Saturday nights. Seldom get an Alert now, but feel that there is more to come to us.

<u>14th May 1943</u>

Get regular letters from Gerald in Ceylon. He says he is reminded of the illustrations in <u>Little Master!</u>* [Other local boys later said the same.] Went to a meeting in London for relatives of his Regiment, 115 Field Regiment RA. Last weekend rejoicing over Tunisian victory. Simply awestruck at sudden collapse of Germans. Now we wait.

The weather has turned warm and everything looks so beautiful. The East Park is nearly all cultivated now and a wonderful sight with wheat and oats. The clearing of the hawthorn bushes was done by Italian prisoners. It is grand to see it productive and not a rabbit warren. The warren itself is sown with oats. Am busy with my tame rabbits, helping the Food Front.

Strange to hear the bombers go out on their big raids at night. They usually seem to go over here when going to Italy. One Sunday night about a month ago they streamed out in three lines for $1^1/_2$ hours, very high up, not a plane to be seen, the sound swinging back and forth till it seemed the air was moving in great waves. The head and tail of each lot was lit up – this in itself was a thrill in the blackout.

People realise that the next months will see more casualties than we have had so far. God speed the right and the end of it all. Mr Churchill is in Washington again!

<u>May 1943</u>

Dam busting by RAF – Wing Commander Guy Gibson. Glorious weather. Terrible raids on Germany and Italy. Mr Eden

(<u>Little Master, A Story of Ceylon</u>, by A. Kathleen Shorten, illustrated by J.M. Muriel Carlile and H.E. Payne. Church Missionary Society. Read by ET to the Sunday School, about 1927.)*

in Portsmouth said we would take no notice of people who thought bombing awful. They were silent when we were getting it.

June 1943

Lemons and bananas offered in ones to be raffled for Wings for Victory Weeks etc and making enormous sums – brought from Tunisia or America. Children do not know what a banana is or how to eat it.

8th and 9th June 1943

WI Annual General Meeting in Albert Hall, first held since 1939. We had a surprise when the Queen arrived. She walked down the central aisle where I was a steward, so I had a front stalls view. She looked very lovely in pale lavender grey with turned-up hat massed with little blue and mauve flowers – and her beautiful pearls. She made a charming speech and remained for about an hour while Mr Hudson (Minister of Agriculture) and Lady Denman (Chairman) spoke. When going away she was cheered vociferously and then the audience sang 'For she's a jolly good fellow.' The business was very interesting. Resolutions sent in about local government which will probably be of interest in the future as no doubt many women will take part. Anglesey speaker about school meals said they were started in the deep Depression, mainly by WIs, and now 60% take them.

19th June 1943

Fire-watching. Planes going out for over an hour. Stood on the terrace. Beautiful night with full red moon rising – the sea glimmering in the harbour and great gun-flashes occasionally. Several heavy explosions during the night, one expected the windows in again. Alert between 1 and 2, no noise. Planes coming back about 4. Thought 'they' might repeat the trick of coming in with ours with lights on, and drop bombs, as they did lately.

20th June 1943

F. and M. here to supper: sliced tinned ham, salad of lettuce and tomatoes, peas, potatoes, newberry tart, cream from F. Had a joint of beef today and some liver, will make liver sausage.

Feel a state of suspense keying one up these days. Reading about Dunkirk three years ago. We had gritted our teeth and were ready to face anything. We only realise now how terrible were the odds and remember with thankfulness the boys who fought on in that glorious summer weather – the sound of the squadrons of Jerrys and the scream of falling planes.

25th June 1943

Warm weather. Haying everywhere. Oats and wheat already turning, never remember them so early. Our planes roaring over Chichester. Counted a hundred while I waited for a bus.

This month saw the film 'Pygmalion'. Leslie Howard, goodbye.*

5th July 1943

To Portsmouth – Dig for Victory Week. Drove to Westbourne and took bus. On Saturday, gardening Brains Trust – Freddie Grisewood was Question Master. Tom took part. Yesterday had job collecting herbs to take to Up Park where there is a drying station. Back of car filled with camomile. Amazed to see rough ground on way to Chalton now bearing crops of wheat and barley, and good ones. Also at Up Park what had been bracken-covered land now 'ripe to harvest.' Hope the future will remember the land and its goodness in time of trouble. When it comes down to brass tacks we could do without Stock Exchanges and munitions – everything but the earth which gives us life. I don't think many

**(He was lost in an airliner from Lisbon, shot down by the Germans, who apparently thought Churchill was on board.)*

people realize this, especially those living in towns.

Reading The Gobi Desert, in parts like some wonderful fairytale – one gets right away to another world.

Wonder what was up today. Heard planes going out for an hour, the sound that at night means attack in great strength.

There will be no harvest on Mr Gauntlett's big field this year. It is now an aerodrome. Heart-breaking – but necessary. [It was used by fighters during the invasion of Normandy.]

Church bells now allowed to ring for services, and on the wireless. Got new ration books and identity cards. Excellently managed, worked most smoothly. Queues and seats outside. Mr Brett showed how the forms should be filled in.

An Australian gave a short talk at the WI and made our mouths water. He said they wanted to get back to the time when they had steak and onions for breakfast, chop and tomatoes for lunch, roast beef every day.

14th July 1943

This morning saw 60 four-engined bombers flying in formation – most thrilling. Listening to celebration of Bastille Day in London, Cairo, Algiers. Fine speech by de Gaulle. The crowd spontaneously burst into the Marseillaise, which always reminds me of Martin Harvey as Rouget de Lisle in Dublin, 1912. Very sad description of Paris as it used to be, the Paris I never saw.

16th July 1943

Thousands of frogs, about the size of my little fingernail, crossing the road below Emsworth Lodge this evening.

19th July 1943

Mrs Dunlop telling us that she managed to gather from letters there were 'squeals over there.' [Her husband, the Vicar of

Funtington, Chaplain to the Royal West Sussex Regiment (Territorial) was taken prisoner at Dunkirk.]

Very wet, but rain needed. Hope there won't be too much, to spoil the wonderful harvest.

Rome bombed today after leaflets had been dropped.

5th August 1943

Mr Woolfries just called to say he had a grandson born today – the day we captured Catania and the Russians got Orel.

12th August 1943

WI afternoon meeting at Mrs Hair's lovely garden – filled with flowers and the water slipping over the watercress beds. Mrs Grey Wornum spoke, most amusing.

There is to be a ban on travelling in this district. Extraordinary rumours going about. To be or not to be? [Second Front.] If it comes we are likely to know more.

16th August 1943

Sharp raid from 12 to 1 last night on Portsmouth. Heard it was on the Whale Island guns. Heard a shell scream over and go plonk in the East Park or nearer. While the All Clear was sounding a crowd of planes went over. Tom said, "It sounds just like the others" – and down came a bomb (on South Holt.) Almost immediately the Alert went again, and as the All Clear was sounding planes came over and heavy firing started again. A third Alert went soon after, at 2 a.m., but things were quiet after that. In the evening we heard bombers going out – we thought to Italy. They returned some time about 5. Feel rather limp today. Most glorious day. At breakfast time about 60 bombers and attendant fighters went out – later I counted 56 bombers and about 50 fighters back – so someone got it. This evening about 7 an Alert went and firing started towards Portsmouth. Could hear Jerry so went to the back door with glasses. White puffs in the sky (anti-aircraft?) and the heavy guns going, but they could not get on the plane. Just then I heard the engine stop and a moment later saw it falling as a red spot far away. Reconnaissance?

Last night when no guns were firing I heard a Jerry coming and the powerful searchlight at French's Farm went up and almost immediately got it and followed it. Heard it was shot down. Six were brought down out of 25.

8th September 1943

What a day! One to be remembered. Italy has surrendered.

Had a very pleasant relatives' meeting (Gerald's Regiment) at YWCA in London. So much more friendly sitting round tables and having quite a nice tea. Marjorie played for us, ending with 'God Save the King' at 5.30. After, I found that this was just the time of General Eisenhower's broadcast from Algiers announcing the armistice in Italy. Tom said when he met us, "Isn't the news great?" but reminded us of the likely repercussions (Balkans etc.) There were two soldiers in the train and I heard one say, "The Major was nearly knocked out by the news." Hope it is the day which brings nearer their all coming home. Great Russian news too – the Germans out of the Donetz Basin.

16th September 1943

Fierce fighting at Salerno. Germans report we have been forced back – but this evening we are advancing. Enemy making full use of radio. Most incidents are just too 'Buchan' to be true – the story of Mussolini's escape or rescue. Last night the planes went out high overhead in unending procession for over two hours, the air full of vibration. I had a bad headache so noticed it. They were over Germany and occupied countries: "You're telling us," we feel like saying to the announcer. Tonight the same noise has lasted over an hour. There is a great fascination in going out to look at the planes. Nothing to be seen, they fly very high – but sometimes one is lit up. One evening in summer when they were going out to Italy we saw them like great black birds, in threes, but now we only trace the lines by the sound.

Just now when listening at the door I thought I heard a little 'nattering' sound. It may have been a toad, there are dozens about, from wee ones about the size of a fingernail to large grown-ups.

Dozens of convoys on the roads. They removed the mirror at Middle Lodge [blind corner] and cracked it putting it back.

18th September 1943

Roar of planes overhead, fighters skimming the treetops, and Vic Oliver prattling on the wireless – such a contrast! Mussolini has just been produced at the microphone. Food shortage in Bengal and famine – and the next item on the news is what won the St Leger.

8th December 1943

Momentous days. General Smuts's speech: many home truths. Meeting of Stalin, Roosevelt and Churchill at Teheran; Churchill, Chiang Kai Chek and Roosevelt in Cairo. Now Inonu of Turkey, Churchill and Roosevelt are meeting in Cairo and have been joined by Smuts. I wonder what we shall think of their pronouncements twenty years hence.

New Forest Side and Stansted WI – programme arranging here today. Gerald moved to India. Wonder if it will mean Burma.

Marvellous displays of searchlights. Terrible raids all November on Berlin.

Ridiculous hysteria over Mosley's release.

Christmas Eve 1943

A lovely sunny day. Went over to Middle Lodge with sunflower heads for fowls. Yesterday heard carol singers in Westbourne with a flashlight and accompanied by a melodeon. Rode home by Aldsworth, two miles, not a soul on the road. All morning the bombers have gone out. I thought – 'Poor boys … on Christmas Eve.' Some Canadian soldiers said, "What a Christmas for some one."

Listened to 'Scrooge' on the wireless. Very lonely here. Shades of long ago! It is like the ghost of Christmases past – only our kitchen as usual looks 'stirred up with a stick.' Tom doing the crossword and I knitting socks for Tony. I wonder of course where all the boys are and what they are doing?

I have made a cake and iced it. Marzipan made of soya flour, sugar, lots of almond essence. White icing made of milk powder and sugar. Some violet petals and shreds of pre-war angelica. We have a goose so are lucky.

26th December 1943

F. and M. to supper – cold goose and salad, mince pies, jelly (one precious packet left) with home-bottled fruit.

Tonight we heard the names of the new C-in-Cs for the Second Front. People keep saying it will be over by next Christmas. It seems they have the belief that a miracle will happen.

End of the King's broadcast speech: "In the words of a Scottish writer of our day, 'No experience can be too strange and no task too formidable if a man can link it up with what he knows and loves.'" John Buchan.

31st December 1943

New Year's Eve. May 1944 do as well for us – but it will be bitter we know.

St Valentine's Day 1944

A week of pessimism about Italy. News better today. Planes over Continent. Saw Thorney flarepath brilliantly lighted last night. On Thursday as bombers were streaming out heard the scream of a falling plane and saw it fall, a ball of fire over Emsworth way. Hear it was a collision, both crews lost.

Saw a grey wagtail on Westbourne stream in January, coot on mill stream last week and hawk overhead. Violets in the old orchard a month ago. Crocuses and snowdrops in the churchyard under the window. What pleasure one gives to generations by planting snowdrops. I wonder if the clump still flowers near the beech hedge in Ireland, where I watched it for years.

Will there be a second front? Everyone waits. Home Guard called out on unexpected exercise.

Tom goes to London tomorrow. He is being made AHRHS. I have two meetings in Chichester.

25th February 1944

Raids again. Heavy gunfire and incendiaries, but not near. Wonderful searchlights. Heard end of service last night, 'Peace perfect peace', and the guns roaring overhead. Very cold, 14° of frost last night. Glad of bright sunshine.

My evacuee has left to get married to her French Canadian.

6th April 1944

About ten days ago the dome room at Lumley's Seat was burnt out.

Last night the planes went out for over an hour. Still nearly daylight at 9 p.m. with a bright moon. In 1940 and 1941 it was the roar of Germans coming in that we heard: but never in such strength. The Russians are doing marvellously, nearly at Odessa, and we bombed Ploesti oilfields yesterday.

Don't like Imphal situation.

Lots of silver paper about (dropped by planes). Some Germans over one night lately. We suddenly heard a sickening roar as of a falling plane. It recovered and went on: heard it dropped bombs at East Marden, doing no damage.

Great work going on, concreting roadsides, woodland drives, crossroads etc. (parking places for tanks and army vehicles.) Have been asked to volunteer to go anywhere nursing, but how can I? – much as I want to. Coastal ban on travel again imposed. No travel to Ireland.

Tony was 26 last Monday, and I was 26 when he was born in Waterford, with youngsters in the streets outside singing 'Up Johnny Redmond – to Hell with de Valera.' [John Redmond was MP for Waterford.]

Still we wait tensely. Lovely spring, daffodils out for Easter and banks of violets smell so sweet in the orchard. Tremendous convoys on all roads. Americans everywhere, and the sound of their voices as if some had stepped down from the screen – "Say Mam" – "You're tellin' me" – "Thanks a lot." I love to hear the accents of the different States.

Tony has just sent Tom a bottle of whiskey, a great treat – it is 25/9 now.

Still fire-watching on Saturday nights, intensified rules.

25th April 1944

Lovely weather. Raid about 11-1 last night, great noise and gunfire. Hear damage and death in Portsmouth. John, RAF, home last night from Italy. About 11 this morning, watching planes through the fieldglasses, one started to roll. It flashed through my mind, "The Victory roll" and then, "It's too low" – then realised it was slowly falling. I could see fragments falling off the plane and thought one was a parachute – but it didn't open. Heard the crash of falling pieces and went into the deep recess of the Chapel west door. I waited for the crash, but it was quite a dull bang. When Hector and I got up to the edge of the cricket field nothing was to be seen but smoke rising from the beech trees. It had fallen in the Rough Ride. Poor fellows. It had been a collision and the other fell at Idsworth – both killed. A huge piece of plane wing fell across the beautiful clump of whitebells in my front garden. I was lucky it didn't hit me – it was terribly splintered. Nurse felt she must go and see the pilot, but of course there was nothing to be done. Poor John saw it all and was first on the spot – a sad beginning to his leave: but they must be used to death in all forms.

Miss N. told me there are pontoons in the harbour at Emsworth or Bosham [a boat building dock].

<u>26th April 1944</u>

Tremendous air fleet went out tonight, the heaviest vibration I've heard. Alert about 1.40–2.40 and again at 3.30 a.m. Bomb fell on road near Horndean. Hear of the great concentrations of stuff and wonder we don't get more raids. Everyone keyed up for anything. It is strange at night when the gunfire is loudest to hear owls hooting as if in derision and the peewits calling sweetly – and now a nightingale singing. Then in the morning we woke to a perfect April day. Warmth stolen from summer and the trees quickly leafing, the cherry in full bloom and the pink buds of the apple opening. All day in a deep blue sky planes roared. What must it be like on the Continent?

<u>6th May 1944</u>

6° of frost – enough to destroy a good deal of the fruit crop. Along the Chichester road such a lot of blossom is brown, and now the Food Ministry is warning of a likely shortage of fruit. Spent an hour helping to cover the strawberry crop with straw, think it has escaped very serious damage – a lovely crop.

A Typhoon fell near Woodberry Lane. The poor fellow was killed – too low for his parachute to open. The houses there escaped very luckily. Planes going out day and night in most lovely weather, like Dunkirk time.

8th May 1944

Tony walked in for 24 hours looking very fit, said goodbye … a lovely May day in England, the trees just green and the wistaria beginning to come out.

17th May 1944

Bitterly cold with rain and hail. The central heating ban has been lifted all over the country. Several Alerts this week, 'concentrated raid on Portsmouth' on May 15th the Germans say. Terrific gunfire. The guns at Forest Side went off with huge cracks. I hate to hear the Jerrys bumbling about and dread one coming down. Bombs at Bosham killed four horses. An American Liberator fell on a laundry in Chichester, killing three people and damaging hundreds of houses. It was a miracle there were not a lot more killed, as the bombs were still on board and exploded. I saw one of its engines driven through the wall of St John's School in The Hornet. The crew baled out over Bognor – OK. The pilot stayed on and set its course for the sea, but it turned inland after he baled out. He escaped with a broken ankle.

There is one-way traffic on many roads, and driving the car is fraught with much difficulty. Have to carry identity cards always. Roads lined with tanks and if they move they are so ungainly they strike terror into one. The drive through Stansted is closed to us, the Park and forest a vast camp, and we have to go round by French's Farm. One-way traffic in Rowlands Castle, no road to the station from the Arches, so have to go round by Bow Hill.

Westbourne is one-way too, and many roads closed altogether at times, so home is the best place these days.

The wistaria on our house is one mass of flowers. Cold nights kept it from coming out quickly, and now cold days are prolonging the flowering season. Had a parcel from Gerald in India, 1 tin of butter, 1 tin marmalade, 1 lb tea, a packet of Lux, which is not made here now. All most acceptable.

Everyone has a feeling of tension waiting for the opening of the second front. A lot of London conferences cancelled, also WI AGM and Regimental relatives' meeting. Now there is a notice that there will be fewer trains.

Tom has been busy marking 400 exam papers for the National Diploma of Horticulture. He hopes to go to Wisley for the viva voce exams in the first week in June.

27th May 1944

Saturday. Fire-watching – first night for months we had an Alert. There was a continuous rattle of windows before the Alert and all through it. Saw big flashes to the east and flares over Thorney. Heard after there were raids on Brighton and Weymouth, and the window vibration was from terrific bombing across the Channel. Same thing again on Sunday night, and heavy gunfire Portsmouth and Fareham way. One plane over, pursued by searchlights and hellish noise. Was glad when it had passed on.

29th May 1944

Whit Monday. The RAF had a cricket match here this evening, white shirts v. blue shirts. It seemed like old times to see and hear it, and to see Hector batting – he got the biggest score for our side.

Curious to hear night sounds from our south bedroom window, with a wide view down to the sea and over Thorney aerodrome.

Tonight heard jackdaws shrieking, owls and peewits calling, and a steam train puffing along on the Emsworth line. It has just struck 2.

The glory of the wistaria has now departed and I am left with drifting petals floating in every window. All Clear now, 2.10 a.m.

<u>5th June 1944</u>

John Woolfries here for four days' leave, got up a cricket match this evening against the RAF. Saw him batting and twirling his bat – it seemed so like old times and yet not the same – how could it be, when the planes roared over in fours, going out to the Continent. It didn't seem right that some could play cricket and others go out, perhaps to death – but our side had done their day's work towards food production, and John has been 'on ops' since he left us. Went to see the match and luckily took a rug – bitter evening.

<u>6th June 1944</u>

a.m. So it has started.

Kept waking hearing aircraft all night. Heard on the Forces Programme at 9 that Germans said so. Now we hear at 12 noon from London that we have landed in Normandy. Wonder where Tony is.

I am alone – Tom at Wisley for NDH examinations. About 8.30 a.m. went out to look at the squadrons going out in the sun like a shining silver Armada.

I have just realised – <u>it is D-day</u>.

8.45 p.m. For over an hour I have been watching the troop carriers going out, gliding behind the planes as far as the eye could see, north and south, the sky was filled with them. A lifetime seems to have passed since I watched the cricket match last evening, just 24 hours ago – and I'm sure a lifetime's happenings to many of our boys. The BBC observers with the Services gave wonderful descriptions. The fighters have now been screaming out. Heard at 6 that the coast of Normandy has been pounded all day by Naval guns, but we have heard few sounds, I suppose because the wind is north-west, blowing the sound away from us. The King is to speak at 9 p.m. The sun is shining on the masses of scented roses on the roof below the south bedroom and there is a bowl of roses on the table as I write – scent to be for ever associated with D-day. "And that is the end of the News," said Joseph MacLeod – News which lasted nearly an hour. The King, announced by Stuart Hibberd with 'This is London', made an impressive and serious little speech in which he brought together the Queen and every mother in the land tonight. Let us all not expect too much.

It was good to hear the voices of Eisenhower and Monty. I hope today has brought some cheer to people who have so long lived in darkness.

Mrs C. wonders if we shall be attacked tonight – her husband is on Home Guard duty, so I shall go to her if there is any noise.

The planes still fill the sky. Thirty-one thousand airmen were over France today. I wonder if John was! They say our losses have been much smaller than expected – but many have seen their last sunrise. 10 p.m. Went into the Chapel (just a broken shell from the explosion of German bombs in 1940) and as I knelt the fighters were roaring over. The whole place vibrated and twanged, and bits of plaster filtered down. It was musty and dark, all the broken windows canvased up: gone the beauty of that little building, the black-and-white floor and the lovely blue and gold of the chancel ceiling, the unique east window with symbols of the Jewish faith – that has been shattered too. Before the war, American visitors used to knock at our door politely asking if they might see 'where Keats went to church.'* Now it is all a ghost of the past.

*[*See chapter 17, The Chapel and John Keats, in Lord Bessborough's book Enchanted Forest (1984). The Chapel was restored in 1947 by H.S. Goodhart-Rendel and reconsecrated by the Bishop of Chichester, Dr George Bell.]*

Now the big ponderous planes are coming back. The air is alive with noise and the fighters fly outward into the pink-tipped clouds. I must call it a day. All my life I have gone through times of crisis alone. Have spoken to no one all day except at our WI committee meeting here.

[Later we heard that mats made of chestnut spars were used on the beaches for landing army vehicles, and that Mr Churchill had got this idea from seeing chestnut fences being made in Stansted forest.]

7th June 1944

Went to Portsmouth. No police at the station demanding identity cards – the need is over. Strangely quiet. Few civilians about, or traffic – absolutely no Navy. Saw soldiers fully equipped marching along the Common, which is all wired off, so I didn't even see the sea. Surprising there was no attack here – quite expected an air war. And the armada that went out from Portsmouth was not attacked by planes either. Rather different from Dunkirk four years ago! No balloons up over the city or port. Dev Anand (journalist) said they could see the assembly in the harbour the other night, so I expect a lot of Portsmouth people knew and saw it – but there was not a word. It is strange to feel we were in the centre of it all.

Tony's suitcase [sent home when he embarked] has been at Rowlands Castle station since yesterday. He must have known when he wrote on Friday.

8th June 1944

Squadrons started going out at daylight – four-engined bombers, and high above the streaks in the sky showed fighters were there. Through it all, on the topmost bough of the cedar tree, a cock blackbird keeps on singing. I expect his mate is on a nest somewhere near.

Wet and grey this evening. I wonder where T and J are. Heard Bayeux taken today. The tapestry has been removed. By whom? Read some years ago that the Normans were stubborn Resisters. They seem to have given us a welcome.

(Nora, one of the girl gardeners, was on leave last month with her husband. Alas, he was killed on D-day.)

22nd June 1944

Last week the Flying Bomb appeared, to try and lower our morale! Poor Londoners, and others on the south coast. On Monday morning we heard one – it passed over Westbourne, too low for us to see it, and I hear it crashed at Bursledon. We have been very lucky here – touch wood. We ought to be thankful the Americans are in Cherbourg Peninsula, or we should have had a pasting.

Every good flying day the planes go out. The Spits and Thunderbolts, looking venomous, sometimes laden with bombs under each wing or with rockets, rise from Funtington and turn over here. They either skim just over the cedar tree or wheel down behind the elms, just missing them it seems. They are so continuous today that one only notices the quiet times when there is a short lull. Many hundreds of bombers have just gone over like silver butterflies high up in the evening sunlight. All day my doors and windows vibrate and sometimes shake terribly.

The hedges which have not been trimmed have beautiful long trails of pink wild roses. I wonder if they grow in Normandy? I read of a soldier or sailor who had been across and brought back some Normandy roses to a Frenchwoman here.

Heard from Tony after a fortnight! He is in Normandy. A wonderful letter, typically imperturbable. He asks for a French dictionary, so the old Gasc and the phrasebook go on a journey.

25th June 1944

Sunday. Had just finished a letter to Tony, ending with 'Quiet here,' when three Doodlebugs [flying bombs] went over the house, and two others near the coast. [The noise they made was horrible, and the flames they spurted made one think of an invention of the devil. It gave one tense moments, listening for the cutting-out of the engine, when we knew they would come down and explode. It made one feel very guilty, praying that they would go over – and knowing they were passing on to someone else.]

6th July 1944

Flying bombs have fallen in many places near here, fortunately without loss of life. Tom went up to London on Tuesday to give a talk at the RHS Hall in Vincent Square. He had a very uncomfortable journey. Flying bombs passed over the train and came down not far away. Was nearly three hours going up and coming back – one had fallen on the line near Wimbledon. Quite a lot at his lecture. Alerts were on nearly all the time but no one left.

That evening about 5.30 I was gardening when the Alert went. Could not make up my mind if I heard a plane or a flying bomb, but the guns were firing near so I thought I'd better go indoors. Went up to the south bedroom to look through fieldglasses – realised I must get away from the window, so went and sat on the stairs, and only saved myself from being blown down by grabbing the rail. The guns brought down a flying bomb in the middle of the very big camp in the woods near the Fever Hospital. Fortunately not many there – a big lot had gone out yesterday and a new contingent not arrived. No injuries. Began to get worried when Tom had not arrived. He came about 7.15 – had caught the 3.45, glad to get out of London.

So far the bombs seem to travel along the coast. The noise is very sinister. They are what they are meant to be – morale breakers. Kitty says they seem worse to Londoners that the 'real blitz'. I hope people won't let them get on their nerves – it would be dreadful for us to fail the Services. Weather has been awful, especially for flying. Today better, so fleets going out. Those launching places must be smoked out. [That was, we learnt later, why our planes were over the Pas de Calais every day.] Dakotas carry out supplies and bring back the wounded. Interesting diary letter from Tony. He speaks of bells ringing: must tell him of the Angelus, rung three times a day from Catholic churches.

The coot is still on the mill pond. The swans have hatched four cygnets, a great source of interest to old and young.

22nd July 1944

Yesterday Tom called upstairs, "Revolution in Germany" – unbelievable words! Hopped down to listen. A put-up story to bolster fanaticism for Hitler? But today one wonders if it is more widespread.

Flying bombs still coming over. Rudely awakened last night by one going over very low. Weather is dreadful again – 36 hours' rain in Normandy. Wonder how Tony is: the misery of mud and cold!

24th July 1944

Reading Philip Gibbs's book The Interpreter, about Isolation. Americans are in it now, and don't they look grim. Above the clouds the squadrons still streaming out. Once or twice yesterday I could not remain outside – the sound hurt my eardrums so much.

3rd August 1944

Weather lovely. News from France and Russia good. Americans

pushing on Rennes, Dinard, Vire. Russians near Warsaw and Riga. Squadrons of bombers going and coming here, thousands of them – a wonderfully heartening sight to us.

Heard the autumn song of the robin this evening. Have had a long rest from flying bombs, touch wood, but London is suffering terribly.

23rd August 1944

Paris is free – freed by her own people. I heard the announcement – it was just stunning. Later, cycling past the Free French Camp, felt I must stop and speak to the sentry at the gate – he beamed as we shook hands. They say Marseilles is free too, and Roumania has signed peace with Russia. What a day!

The Dakotas were pouring out and we had a flying bomb and then the Alert.

4th September 1944

Brussels is free! Events move so fast these wonderful days. No flying bombs on London since Friday. Mrs C's sister from London sleeping here. Our troops are moving up the flying bomb coast and great explosions are heard in Kent from there.

Did not hear from Tony for two weeks until today. He says American rations are marvellous, especially the coffee.

Busy making jam and bottling fruit. For the past fortnight the wireless news has been like something we dreamed about. Delighted to hear that General Montgomery is made a Field Marshal. A great time – but my canny Scots blood keeps me from hurrahing yet.

6th September 1944

Just heard 7 a.m. news. We are in Holland, have taken Antwerp. It is difficult to write of these things while one is living them.

There is a deep feeling of thankfulness among the English people – no hilarity – it is all too near.

The beaches are open again and a generation of children enjoying the sea for the first time. Personally I shouldn't care to bathe yet. Too many mines, especially after the stormy weather. We have had gales for three days. Two lots of visitors from the flying bomb areas sleeping here. They had not slept in a bed for weeks – upper rooms too badly damaged. They have been in shelters or sleeping under tables. What a problem confronts the authorities, to get even <u>mending</u> of houses done.

<u>17th September 1944</u>

Wonderful news of air armada to Holland. Thousands of gliders. We did not see these (low down behind the trees.) Later – Arnhem. Wonder where Tony is.

<u>20th September 1944</u>

Many people with children returning to London. A great pity, as bombs are still coming (V2s).

Strange item in Tony's last letter. He opened a letter addressed to Captain W. Tomalin (his initials are W.A.) and it was one written in London to Uncle Will, with American forces in New Guinea!

Planes keep going out – but the war is drifting away from us now.

<u>1945</u>

Christmas passed quietly. John had leave. It was like old times to go to Middle Lodge on Christmas evening. Ardennes breakthrough. Great Russian drives. Hear regularly from Gerald [in Burma] and Tony [in Belgium], both in front lines.

10th–19th February 1945

Tony had leave. Monday 19th, heard John missing. Mrs Woolfries did not want Tony to know and only let me know after he had gone. Hoping all the time.

6th March 1945

Still no news of John, but as he wirelessed he had landed safely, feel he is alive and may be hiding or a prisoner. Tony went back into the big push to the Rhine. Wonder if he is near Wesel [where the Germans were retreating across the Rhine]. It must have been awful to go back to it all. Felt for him but of course said nothing. One never goes behind the mask they wear.

Heard today Gerald is in the 19th Indian Division on the Irawaddy Bridgehead. He writes so cheerfully, it must be an effort sometimes. Study every map given in the Times and try to follow the war in Burma. [But – with events in Europe there was a certain amount of truth that they were a 'forgotten army' – though not by people whose sons were there. Thanks to our Ministry of Information our part was unknown to Americans – hence the 'Objective Burma' film which depicted Burma taken by a handful of American parachutists. The journalists knew. All praise to the Allies, all of them – they fought a bitter fight.]

Piloted planes are again raiding England, and long-range V-bombs. Shall we be in it again. Always feel they will make one terrible last smash, gas or something.

Churchill met Eisenhower and Monty, and was in Germany – sent a shell with greeting to Hitler. Rather playing down to popularity? I wonder if Ray (in the Middle East) will soon be home. I think of all the boys always when Big Ben strikes 9, saying to the chimes, "May God be with us and our Allies." [Heard in Holland in 1950 how much Big Ben and the BBC meant to them.]

24th March 1945

Montgomery has crossed the Rhine at Wesel – and the Navy was there! Mystified until we heard how the great craft had been brought overland. Mr Churchill over there. He had to be in it. Don't blame him, but glad he's safely back.

2nd April 1945

Monday. Heard tonight no V-bombs since Thursday. Is London free?

No news of John, but hoping, as we hear of the Germans' evacuating Holland. Heard the weather bulletin on the wireless for the first time since before the war. Ray to be home soon, and Forest Side boys, after nearly five years.

April-May 1945

Berlin almost conquered. Things seem moving to a close so fast that one listens and looks on rather in a daze. Mussolini executed by Italians. Good riddance, but people said they hated the brutality of his end. Tony in Holland. Gerald coming home on leave! (Under LIAP – 'Leave In Advance Of PYTHON' (Repatriation)).

Russians and Americans have met. The stories of the terrible concentration camps bring home the truth.

Prisoners returning all over the district. Home Office booklet on VE Day. Wonderful to be able to look forward.

4th May 1945

At 9 p.m. Frank Phillips read the News, but did not say "Read by FP" – first time since 1940. The news was – the surrender of all Germans in Holland, North Germany, Denmark, at 8 a.m. tomorrow the 5th. Yesterday great surrenders. The day before, Hitler's death. (Hero or suicide?) Surrender in Italy and part of Austria.

Today the 14th Army take Rangoon! We are dazed – drugged with tremendous happenings. Even when Hitler's death was announced I noticed no elation. How can one rejoice when so many won't come back? and when one realises the agony of thousands who have been tortured.

The blackout is over and today I saw a boy flying a kite – this was not allowed during the war. Ice cream has been made for about a month now. Oranges fairly plentiful since Christmas.

6th May 1945

Only Tony to write to. Gerald on the way home from Burma. For nearly five years have written to both every Sunday evening.

7th May 1945

Unconditional surrender signed at Rheims. Mr Churchill to speak tomorrow at 3 p.m. and the King at 9. So tomorrow is VE Day at last! The garden men are not very anxious to take the two days' holiday. If it is fine they feel they ought to be planting potatoes – such a tyrant is Nature.

We have had our supper of soup and an egg for a treat. Don't feel like drinking toasts tonight with no one to join in. Even Tom, always so ready, hasn't suggested it very forcibly. I think of the Woolfries and others whose sons have not yet come home. Wonder where the boys are?

Have just had a walk along the lawns. Very warm, moist and quiet; only the peewits calling and late rooks settling in their nests.

May 1945

John came back! One night about 11 p.m. his brother-in-law rang Stansted House with news of his arrival. He had not been heard of for months. Lord and Lady Bessborough and Lady Moyra went to tell his parents, and Mr Holloman, the chauffeur, came to tell us – we all just had to drink his health, then dashed over to see the Woolfries.

He looked so different when he came. One could see he had had a bad time. Later – his old self again.

Gerald walked in one night. He came from beyond Mandalay (captured in March) by jeep to an airfield; flew to Chittagong; by train to Calcutta and Karachi; flew to Bahrein, Cairo, Sidi Barrani, in hospital Dakotas with stretcher cases, other passengers sitting on the floor; then via Malta, over Italy and France, landing at Hendon; got to Rowlands Castle station at midnight and walked up the long Avenue, past Middle Lodge, through the beeches and over the cricket field. He met no one on the way, but early next morning Mrs Woolfries sent over some eggs for his breakfast. Later I asked how she knew he'd come.

"I woke up and heard someone open the little gate into the Park – and then turn back."

The West Park was ploughed up two years ago and is now a field of barley.

Appendix 1

Prisoner of war, 1945

Squadron Leader John Woolfries, RAF

As regards my experiences when I was shot down there is nothing much to reveal except to say that the details are always pretty vivid in one's mind.

We were stationed at Vokel in Holland and on 10 February 1945 I was attending an Escape and Evasion lecture when I was called out and briefed to take my flight to look for enemy movement towards the Rhine as the Allies were shortly to attempt a crossing. I remember the Army Intelligence officer saying to my Squadron IO, "You shouldn't have told him about the crossing, what if he gets shot down?" to which we both replied, "Don't be bloody stupid."

We flew in flights of four aircraft at 8000 feet, the best height to avoid flak. Not long after take off one returned, with only two aircraft to manoeuvre and to get a closer look at roads and railways I went lower. Suddenly I saw on a railway siding a few rail trucks and immediately knew it was what we called a 'Flak Trap.' The Germans used these as bait, they were actually full of A.A. guns. I turned but too late as there was a loud bang and I was covered in hot oil. I instructed my No. 2 to come in and lead me home as I couldn't see.

By this time it was getting rather warm inside the old Tempest, and because of fire I switched the engine off – as there was only one I couldn't very well go anywhere, only down, which was rather unfortunate as I was just north of Wesel and we were not over-popular with the Germans at that particular time.

I jettisoned the hood and side panels – when you have done

this on a Tempest it's almost like sitting up there on a horse. The idea was to bail out, but when I looked at the ground I realised I was too low, so I decided to land in a nice little field with houses and a farm on two sides and a wood on the third side. My radio was still working so I called the other two aircraft and told them I was all right and would try and escape. Ha, Ha, Ha.

For a moment I thought of blowing up the aircraft, but decided I was very close to the houses and if I was caught they wouldn't have been too pleased with me blowing up their village. I ran like hell for the wood, and when I had covered about 100 yards I saw a little man in civilian clothes beckon me. I ran over to him thinking he was a Pole or some other Forced Labour worker who would help. As I reached him the dirty devil pulled a revolver on me. We were soon surrounded by German soldiers and I was marched off to what I thought was the local school. Not long after this the SS arrived. I thought then that I had had it.

Their interrogation through an interpreter was very poor. It had not lasted long before the Luftwaffe in the form of an armed Warrant Officer, plus bicycle, came to my rescue. He took me off to the local gaol. On the way the thought went through my mind to overpower him, but as there was snow on the ground I thought I would be easily tracked, so discretion got the better part of valour.

I spent a miserable night in this gaol and next day was taken to the airfield at Wesel.

I spent about two or three days there being looked after quite well.

A little Russian boy used to come each day and wave to me, giving the thumbs-up sign. He boosted my morale no end. I wonder what happened to him?

I was then taken to the Interrogation Centre at Frankfurt. We travelled by train, being caught in a raid at Essen. It was a bit dicey being in an air raid shelter with a bunch of German civilians – when the bombs started falling some of their looks were not exactly friendly. My escort spoke perfect English and was of course supposed to get information out of me. I had a feeling he might have been persuaded to take me in the opposite direction from Frankfurt, towards the Rhine, as he made it fairly obvious that he realised they had lost the war. I of course didn't trust him, and thought had I suggested it he might have smelt a rat about the Rhine crossing.

At Frankfurt Interrogation Centre, or the 'Sweat Box', as it was known by the RAF, one is put into a small bare cell with one window, too high to see out of, the only furniture being a bed with wooden slats and one threadbare blanket. As it was very cold, the cell was made very hot during the first part of the evening, and then just as one gets to sleep the heat is turned off and you wake up shivering. It remains this way for the rest of the night, depriving one of any sleep, the idea being to soften one up for interrogation.

I spent about ten days at Frankfurt being periodically taken from my cell for interrogation. They tried all sorts of tricks to get one to talk, such as offering alcohol and cigarettes, or threatening to hand you over to the Gestapo. I remember on one occasion the most obvious German I have ever seen, dressed in a brown suit, being ushered into my cell saying he was the Swiss representative of the Red Cross. When I refused to answer his questions he stormed out saying, "I suppose you think if you answer my questions Montgomery will have to alter his plans."

Eventually, with others, mostly American, I went by train to Stalag VII (I think) near Nuremberg. It was a bit frightening when American Mustangs flew over us, but some clever chap had written P.O.W. on top of the coaches, so they didn't strafe us. Not long before, I had shot up every train we saw.

The main snag in Stalag VII was hunger. I was in charge of a hut which contained 140 Americans, mostly enlisted men, Air Gunners etc., who were pretty tough. The few officers were jolly good types. After about a month we received Red Cross parcels which were a Godsend. Then the thieving started and I had to take pretty tough measures to stop it.

Eventually the Germans decided that the Allies were getting too close and the whole camp should be moved further south, and so the long march began. By this time my flying boots had holes in them, and I began to think I would be walking in bare feet. Luckily the night before the move I had ten British Army Sergeants allotted to join my 140 Yanks. These chaps had been prisoners since Dunkirk and were absolutely wonderful. They soon produced a stout pair of Army boots for me and off we went.

On the first day we were bombed by the Americans and six chaps were killed, but after that they obviously realised their mistake and on lots of days American fighters gave us a friendly look.

The motley rabble consisted of well over a thousand prisoners. We slept in churches, farm buildings and in the open. There was still snow on the ground and to keep warm at night two or three of us would huddle together. We did get the occasional Red Cross parcel, and we supplemented this by pinching the odd chicken and eggs when we slept at a farm. My 140 were like a herd of sheep. They wouldn't do a thing without asking me. I got completely fed up with their cries of "Captain Woolf" as they called me.

We eventually arrived at Moosberg near Munich, which had been a Concentration Camp. I saw some of the political prisoners being marched out as we arrived. They were walking skeletons. Moosberg was full of Americans, Russians and British. At one time all RAF officers were segregated to be taken away as hostages, but luckily Himmler refused to carry out the Führer's order.

I met many old friends, one who I had seen shot down over Crete many years before had the situation well in hand as he spoke perfect German.

General Patton and his boys eventually arrived at the end of April. The Germans went out to meet him under a flag of truce, to ask if he would wait for 48 hours to allow the prisoners to be escorted behind Ally lines. He quite rightly said "No", as 48 hours would have given the Germans time to improve the defences of Moosberg. The SS then took all our guards who refused to fight, put them in the Guardroom and threw hand grenades through the door. The battle for Moosberg took place between the two armies, the Germans occasionally lowering their guns to pepper us up.

Eventually Patton arrived, complete with low slung pearl handled pistols, and all hell broke loose. The Russians much to our annoyance burnt down the brewery in the town and killed all the pigs in a local farm.

We waited around, the war ended and still the Yanks hadn't got us home. Eventually we were flown to France and the RAF took over. In no time we arrived in England, on 10 May 1945, the organisation being terrific.

The three months I did as a prisoner was unpleasant and frustrating, but in many ways probably did me a lot of good. It taught me to appreciate the small things in life. I now know what it is like to go hungry for long periods. I also know what it is like to pick up cigarette ends and roll them in toilet paper, although I have long since given up smoking them. Much to Nancy's annoyance I hate to throw anything away.

I was a fool to be shot down, and realised as soon as I hit the ground that I was operationally tired, having by subterfuge done 50 hours more operations than I should have done on this tour. I did this because I was disappointed – having been taken off operations in mid-1941 to be made a Flying Instructor – at having done only a short tour on a squadron from the end of 1940. As there was no life like being on a Fighter Squadron, I managed to get back in 1943 and vowed never to leave that way of life until the end of the war.

From my point of view it was all worth it – and after all the Belgians did give me the Order of Leopold avec Palme and a Croix de Guerre avec Palme, and in 1955 I was awarded the MBE for services to flying.

Appendix 2

Looking back: Normandy 1944/1951

Major Tony Tomalin, London Welsh Regiment

In May 1951 I returned from East Africa on six months' leave after more than three years in Tanganyika. Unlike those living in England I knew I should be allowed to buy a car immediately. I was determined to have another look at Bayeux and the Normandy beaches, and I thought I would take my wife with me, but was doubtful whether she would be enthralled – and so was she!

However, a letter arrived saying that a party from the Regiment was to take the trip, organised by Donald Harries and "Hooky" Payne. The idea was to make a beginning this year by visiting the Gun Sites in Normandy on which the Regiment had deployed after landing on the beaches.

On 14th October 1951 Donald and I met Hooky at Dover and were soon in a bar going over old times: from the very old times of 303 in London during the 1940 raids, to the Orkneys, Pembroke, Leeds battle training, mobile training, depot battery at Larkhill, Barnsley, Canterbury and Southend. On the crossing to Boulogne I asked Donald about the bombing of the ship in which he and the Commanding Officer and others of the Regimental Recce party crossed to Arromanches. I hadn't heard this story before. It seems the ship was hit fair and square, with many casualties and much damage, and the Regiment was lucky to possess a Colonel and second-in-command when it landed. I told Donald of our LST journey from Tilbury down the North Foreland with destroyer escort, through the Straits of Dover with all ships and escorts putting out a heavy smoke screen, westwards through the

Channel hugging the coast, until at dusk we turned south and headed for Normandy. I recalled the "E" boat attack which left one ship behind in flames, several false alarms when enemy aircraft in large numbers were thought to be approaching, and everyone's astonishment when dawn broke and we found ourselves off the French coast in the middle of an unbelievable conglomeration of shipping.

While we talked our boat neared Boulogne, the entrance to which is much the same today as it must have been seven years ago when the war swept past it. One incident struck me: meat bones were thrown from the ship's galley to the dogs on the quay, where they were somewhat languidly disputed. Seven years ago they would have been seized by hungry urchins and the dogs wouldn't have had a look in.

After lunch at the café Liegeoise behind the harbour – I will try to spare you the pain of descriptions of the delicious food (in 1951 food rationing was still in force) – we decided to call at the site north of Rouen where the Regiment had halted during the advance from Normandy to Ostend. We visited the woods which 318 had chosen as their wagon lines, and the V1 launching site dug cleverly into the hill behind the woods, which Hooky told us was still much the same as when they discovered it in 1944.

In Rouen too little had changed. The skeleton of that magnificent cathedral was still there, and although most of the rubble of bomb damage had been cleared away there had been little rebuilding; but there is an air of cheerfulness and prosperity about present day Rouen which we liked.

Next morning we crossed the Seine on the Bailey Bridge, still giving good service, and soon we were passing through the familiar apple orchards of the Calvados country. Lisieux, so heavily bombed and shelled, is still a shattered town, but Caen we found had been greatly rebuilt. We recalled that June day of glorious sunshine in

1944 when we watched the thousand bomber raid on this city, planes passing through a colossal German barrage. Do you remember the bomber which had been badly damaged and, after the crew had baled out, continued to dive and loop in the sky for half an hour until orders were given to shoot it down?

We drove on to Bayeux picturing the scenes we remembered – tank battles, burnt-out wreckage of vehicles (all German transport I recall had red crosses painted on them) the single lines of marching infantry, the endless slowly moving transport, and the wayside graves. The countryside now bears absolutely no hint of those scenes, until one sees an occasional tree with its top cut off.

We had a great welcome from the landlord of the Lion d'Or. Early next day we reached the chateau where Regimental headquarters had been established in the grounds. The dug-out which had housed "Cats" Catterson and the Signals section was still in evidence. At any moment I expected to see Regimental Sergeant Major Chandler emerge from behind a tree and tear strips off an erring gunner ... The reception we got from Mademoiselle was most touching, and as she poured us a glass of wine she said again and again, "Many regiments came here after you but none was as good as the London Welsh."

We called at the chateau at Buhot cross roads which had housed 75 Brigade headquarters and Brigadier "Lofty" Benson, whose familiar figure will be recalled visiting gun sites and Batteries astride a tiny Airborne motorcycle with his long legs sticking above the handlebars. We then turned west and drove through orchards which had been Hooky's headquarters into the farmyard of Camille, whose cheerful red face broke into a welcoming grin as he caught sight of us. Regaling us with wine in the kitchen, he showed us the 3.7 shell with the Regimental crest painted on it, and talked of those days. Hooky misinterpreted to Donald and me such of the conversation as we were unable to follow, but we were all quite fluent by the time the second bottle had been broached. Hooky told us how the Brigade Sergeant Major once almost shot the troop to pieces when he was having a rather keen shot with a Bren Gun at a low flying Jerry plane.

At Crepon we located the "F" Troop Site with the famous airstrip beyond it on which the fighters had landed from England with their auxiliary petrol tanks full of beer for the RAF boys; and beyond that the field hospital. The Gun Site command post and earthworks were still intact, and a few old jerry cans, shell boxes and other rusty pieces had been left in situ by the farmer.

In Bayeux that evening we visited all the cafés of old and had the most impressive dinner, which began with oysters and finished with several glasses of calvados – smooth matured calvados and not the fire water of 1944.

Next morning we set out for 303 Headquarters on the road to St Gabriel and Creully. The small square acre of wood looked just the same, but I forced my way through thick undergrowth to the foxholes that had been Ross's and my own homes in those early weeks. The atmosphere was eerie as I stood in that silent wood beside those old holes in the ground.

The beaches at Arromanches were just as they had been at the time of our landing, without the mass of shipping and the heavy cruiser throwing shells towards the Caen-Bayeux road. French salvage experts were hard at work with flame cutters on the wreckage still littering the beach, and the concrete block ships protecting the Mulberry Port are still there. I drove along the sand and Hooky took ciné film of the scene: reminding me of the LST Captain who came ashore while we were landing and took photographs of our guns and vehicles as they came down the ramp and splashed ashore.

We got back on to the road by one of the concrete runways constructed to serve the Mulberry Quay: and drove slowly through the village of Arromanches, back to Bayeux.

Afterword

1st October 1980

Walked up the Church Path (in the Groves, near the Emsworth Lodge) where dormice were in the 1930s. Hazels, briar bushes and brambles still there. No dormouse nests. Squirrels, grey ones now, had stripped the redwood bark for dreys, as of old. Birds: chaffinches, long-tailed tits, wrens, robins, jays, pheasants.

In the Old Garden: apple trees with many apples. One with the hole where bluetits nested is unchanged, and there was nest material, old moss, inside.

The thin rushy turf around Pitt's Copse is now lush pasture, a herd of black and white bullocks feeding.

30th May 1984

Bright spring day. Cuckoos: six continuous bouts of calls.

Alas: Pitt's Copse cut down, in the middle of the nesting season.

(Jack Pitt was 'a carpenter and jobber' in Stansted woods, playing cricket in his spare time, until he took to highway robbery as Jack the Gunman in the early 19th century. At that time there was an inn, The Packhorse, near the copse, in the Racton Lane; Jack must have lain in wait there for likely customers. Dashing he sounds, but he must have had dark thoughts and fears, and that side of the copse had an eerie atmosphere. He was hanged at Portsmouth in March 1808, aged 27. See: Bourne In The Past by Dr J.H. Mee, 1913.)

25th June 1985

Stansted gardens and grounds now open to the public.

Pyramid orchises in the old site near the Emsworth Lodge drive.

Swallows, chaffinches, greenfinches, goldfinches in the gardens. The Garden Field is now a modern pasture. Trees in the Arboretum are full of nests. Beautiful flower-beds again in the upper garden. Beehives in the young lime grove – the wych elms here, grown old and dangerous, were cut down in the 1970s.

10th September 1985

Twenty tortoiseshell butterflies on sedum by the Tropical House. Bunches of grapes on the muscat vines. Peach and nectarine trees flourishing, and the old fig trees heavy with fruit. Swallows: a great flock (a hundred?) flying around Stansted House, taking midges on the lawns.

Replanting the beeches in the drive: young trees protected by fawn-coloured funnels (polypropylene tree shelters) to keep off deer, squirrels, rabbits. Older trees now in wire netting. Foresters making chestnut fencing.

25th April 1986

Seven loud chiffchaffs by the Church Path, loud warbler in the Old Garden. Many nest-holes in the old apple trees – too soon for eggs this bitter late spring. Splendid daffodils. Wistaria on the garden house just budding. Hector Crockford, the head gardener, saved it in the 1950s by training new suckers when the old tree was dying. Collared doves now calling. Tulip tree planted by Baron de Neuflize (1929) is huge. Also the Queen Mother's oak (1939). Cedars gone from the churchyard. Young beeches flourishing, protective funnels removed. Brimstone butterflies (6), tortoiseshell (2). Pussy-willow on Forest Side hill, always called the 'palm tree', full of bees, one bumble-bee.

7th September 1986

Mustering swallows. Butterflies in the garden: brimstone, red admiral, peacock, tortoiseshell.

22nd April 1987

Glorious day, sun and breezes. Masses of primroses. Long-tailed tit's nest again by the old gorse clump. Cuckoos calling, and loud chiffchaffs.

Peewits over the West Park, kingcups and moorhens by the ponds.

8th September 1987

The great tree damaged by the crashing German plane (8th October 1940) is dying, the top already dead.

Hector talked of the barn owls that used to live in the Chapel tower – from below one could hear them 'snoring'. Young owls once flew in through his bedroom window in the garden house, he had to chase them out.

14th January 1988

(On the night of 15–16th October 1987 a great storm hit the south, especially Sussex.)

Beautiful day, brilliant sunshine, hazel catkins, blackbird singing near the Emsworth Lodge, and many thrushes. Cock pheasants stalking about.

Old oaks at the top of the Church Path untouched. Oaks, cedar and beeches around the Chapel also still there, DG. Trees behind the older cricket pavilion badly hit, and in the drive to Irongate Cottages, and especially in the West Park beechwood; but the new young beeches are flourishing. Ancient cedars in the Arboretum also badly hit, one gone in the Old Orchard – surprisingly, a strong-looking tree. Three young walnuts planted to replace the two old ones.

23rd March 1989

Many clumps of white snowflakes (Leucojum vernum) now by the Chapel – spread from two plants in the 1920s.

8th August 1989

Sweet chestnut and acacias planted in Irongate drive, to replace the losses.

22nd February 1990

Masses of snowdrops in Cooper's Wood.

To see Hector Crockford at Irongate Cottage, and asked about the muscat and black grape vineries in the upper range of glasshouses: how were the vines saved, after the October 1940 plane-crash, when all the lower range were smashed? Answer: the blast missed the top range!

Hector showed me a silver-mounted cricket ball, presented to him by Lord Bessborough after he took ten wickets with it in one match.

14th April 1990

Easter Eve. Pitt's Copse replanted – oaks and wild cherries, in fawn-coloured sheaths. The old hazel and ash-boles remain. Carpeted with primroses and dog violets. One day it will be beautiful again.

9th September 1991

Beehives in the lime grove, young limes flourishing: they flowered this summer. Butterfly count: 40 small tortoiseshells on sedum clump by the Tropical House, 30 on another. Apple-trees now gone from the middle walk, only one peach tree on the east wall; but the old fig flourishing on the west wall. Many bees on flower-beds.

8th April 1992

Celandines, milkmaids, white violets in the lime grove. Bees flying from hives. Orchard daffodils better than ever, hazels and old pear tree budding, new trees planted. Kestrels, brimstone butterflies.

12th April 1992

To Brock Snap. Widespread green hellebore colony – a few plants in 1947.

22nd June 1992

Five pyramid orchises by the Emsworth Lodge drive, as 60 years ago. Parish boundary plaque uncovered behind the fig-tree – we used to hear that the boundary was 'one of the garden paths.'

29th September 1992

Charles, head gardener (he came in 1969) remembers the felling of the wych elm grove, now the lime grove – very deep-rooted, he says.

26th March 1993

The lime grove a 'bee-loud glade.' The old horse chestnut, with nest-holes, seems unchanged. Toad Crossing notice near the Emsworth Lodge.

12th May 1993

Dormice again. Late evening visit to Dot Eaton's dormouse colony in an enclosure at Windsor. Dormice feeding (apples, seeds, beech leaves) scampering on bushes very fast – especially two yearlings – climbing, running upside-down on branches and ceiling, mating, preening (one washed repeatedly over the ears with both paws) scratching, fighting (two males, squeaking, hissing and challenging), eating with great concentration, already quite fat; gazing at us with huge black eyes. Golden brown, delicate fingers, long fuzzy tails, creamy-white undersides, silky fur. So nonchalant and secure, seeming unaware of captivity: and breeding. Fifty of them, including many young. ("Do what one will, it is exceptional for dormice to breed in captivity" – Frances Pitt, naturalist and writer, 1938.) Floreat Dot Eaton.

<u>28th September 1993</u>

Lovely smells – wet mossy woods, oak leaves, heliotrope, buddleia, cedars, yews.

<u>29th August 1994</u>

New hazel grove planted opposite the old one in the Old Orchard.

<u>12th April 1995</u>

Swallows back, also loud chiffchaffs and warbler. No cuckoos yet. Kestrel calling, thrushes and blackbirds singing. Tortoiseshell butterfly, orange tip, bumblebees.

<u>10th September 1996</u>

Green nuts scattered under hazels (grey squirrels). Fruit room open again – plums, greengages, figs.

<u>1st April 1997</u>

Brimstones, tortoiseshells; loud chiffchaffs near Emsworth Lodge, lime grove, Ladies' Mile, Cooper's Wood. Dog violets, strawberry flowers, stitchwort, on the bank beyond the two yews on Forest Side hill. No 'top of the bank' footpath now - made by school children for 100 years: Forest Side school closed about 1960.

Taxi driver, very fond of Stansted, wants it made into a Disney theme park.

<u>10th August 1998</u>

Wonderful smell of box edges in the Middle Walk and Dutch Garden.

<u>29th July 1999</u>

Old frameyard and plantation now a Garden Centre, the Tropical House a restaurant. New Wellhead Garden, fenced from deer.

<u>14th June 2000</u>

Bee orchises, spotted orchises, pyramid, twayblade, protected in grass opposite the estate office; where the bee orchises were in the 1930s.

<u>29th August 2001</u>

Swallows feeding young in Stansted House eaves: eight nests. Old trees flourishing in the Arboretum - three redwoods, magnolia, tulip, mulberry...